THE PRINCESS AND THE TOAD

FOUR ORIGINAL ONE-ACT PANTOMIMES
GORDON HOUSE

Beercott

The Princess and the Toad
Four original one-act pantomimes

First Published in Great Britain in 2025 by Beercott Books.

Text Copyright: © Gordon House 2024
Cover design © Beercott Books 2025

ISBN: 978-1-7393020-8-5

Gordon House has asserted his rights to be identified
as the author of this book.

Title is fully protected under copyright. All rights, including professional and amateur stage production, recitation, lecturing, public reading, motion picture, radio broadcasting, television and the rights of translation into foreign languages are strictly reserved.

A catalogue record of this book is available from the British Library.

No one shall make any changes to the play for the purpose of production without prior written permission from the publisher. No part of this book may be reproduced, stored in a retrieval system, or transmitted in any form, by any means, now known or yet to be invented. This includes mechanical, electronic, photocopying, recording, videotaping, or otherwise, without the prior written permission of the publisher. No one shall upload this title, or part of this title, to social media websites.

Professional and amateur producers are hereby warned that title is subject to a licensing fee. Publication of this play does not imply availability for performance. Both amateurs and professionals considering a production are strongly advised to apply to the agent before starting rehearsals, advertising, or booking a theatre. A licence fee must be paid whether the title is presented for charity or gain and whether or not admission is charged.

Worldwide licence enquiries for this title should be directed to:
licencing@beercottbooks.co.uk.
Title subject to availability.

---

www.beercottbooks.co.uk

Beercott

ACKNOWLEDGEMENTS

Many thanks for their help and encouragement to:

Abbie Andrews, Alan Bennett, Lizzie Burder, Judi Dench, Emily Dyson, Emma Hixson, Stephanie Houtman, Will Howard, Sophia Lorenti, Lucinda Mason Brown, Maria McGurl, Peter Milroy, Phil Newman, Vicky Payne, Sam Peterson, Kristine Pommert, Nathan Rushmer, Charlie Shakespeare, Lucy Sprekley, Angela Thomae, Sarah Tombling, Emma Swan and Tracy Wiles

And particularly to David Chilton for his brilliant music, without which these plays would have been mere bagatelles

And to Peter Wallder for his generosity in giving me a home – Colour House Theatre – to stage these productions, the first of which he also directed

And to Neil Summerville for making the King and the Royal Soothsayer fabulously real!

This book is dedicated to my lovely granddaughters
Celeste, Jessica and Abigail

Gordon House

CONTENTS

PRODUCTION NOTES 9

THE PRINCESS & THE TOAD 11

BEAST 61

RUMPELSTILTSKIN AND THE SLEEPING BEAUTY 111

SNOW WHITE AND THE BIG BAD WOLF 161

ABOUT THE AUTHOR 208

PRODUCTION NOTES

CAST NUMBERS: Each of the four plays is devised for four actors to play at least two distinct roles. (More actors can be used if this doubling is not wanted.)

CHORUS: Made up randomly from actors not otherwise in a particular scene

SONGS: The scripts feature the words for various songs. Originally these were scored by David Chilton. If you enquire about a performance licence you will be informed how to access David's music.

GENERAL NOTES: If a director wants a full evening of pantomime, rather than a single 70 minute play, running any two of these pantos together, with an interval, would work rather well.

THE PRINCESS & THE TOAD

First performance at Colour House Theatre, Easter 2017

ORIGINAL CAST:
KING HORACE/ROYAL SOOTHSAYER : Neil Summerville
QUEEN BEATRICE/WITCH: Emma Swan
PRINCESS SHIRLEY: Stephanie Houtman
PRINCE CYRIL, THE HEAD TOADSMAN/TOAD: Will Howard

SCENES

SCENE 1 - The Royal Throne Room
SCENE 2 - The Royal Toadpool
SCENE 3 - The King's Chamber
SCENE 4 - The Palace Ramparts
SCENE 5 - The Royal Toadpool

PRINCESS AND THE TOAD

SCENE 1 – THE ROYAL THRONE ROOM

The curtain opens to reveal KING HORACE, crown askew and legs dangling over an easy chair, munching his way through a rapidly diminishing pile of muffins. His face is streaked with butter and his shirt sleeves covered in jam. He seems surprised but unconcerned to find himself the centre of attention.

KING: *(noticing the audience)* Ah – hello. Just having a muffin. You can't beat them. Some people prefer toasted teacakes of course – or hot buttered scones dripping with honey - but I've always been a muffin-man myself.

Fancy one, little girl ? You do? Well sorry about that. I'm afraid there are none left! *(and indeed there aren't; the KING has just shoved the last one into his mouth.)* Another time perhaps…

The HEAD TOADSMAN staggers in carrying in a large box marked "TOADS – THIS WAY UP"

HEAD TOADSMAN (HT): Fresh delivery of toads Sire!

KING: *(who can never remember anyone's name)* Ah – wotsyername. I was just telling these good people here that you can't beat a muffin!

HT: At what Sire?

KING: What?

HT: What can't you beat a muffin at Sire? Chess? Snooker? Street Fighter??

KING: No…no you've misunderstood me completely. Listen to this – it's a little song that I've composed. This will explain everything. *(calls out to unseen sound operator)* Give us some music thingy!

Song: KING and CHORUS "You Can't Beat a Muffin"

KING:
(under intro) Oh Yeah!
Oh there's nuffin like a muffin when you're feeling like a snack
Smother it in butter, and there'll be no looking back
Stuff it in your mouth, or lingeringly lick it

Just make sure that no one comes along and tries to nick it

The other cast members dance on to join the KING sing the next two lines

CHORUS AND KING:
You can't beat a muffin

There's absolutely nuffin

KING:
There's nuffin like a muffin every day.

CHORUS:
You can't beat a muffin

There's absolutely nuffin

KING:
I wouldn't have it any other way.

The CHORUS dances as the KING prepares for his second verse

KING:
Now there's folk out there who'd rather have a scone,

A cake or a biscuit- but I think they might be wrong

Add honey on the butter - make sure it's piping hot

A muffin, when it's toasted, is more scrumptious than the lot

CHORUS AND KING:
You can't beat a muffin

There's absolutely nuffin

KING:
There's nuffin like a muffin when it's hot.

CHORUS AND KING:
No you can't beat a muffin

There's absolutely nuffin

KING:
Should anyone deny, they're talking rot!

More exuberant dancing from the chorus

KING:
Oh yeah!

CHORUS:
Oh yeah!

KING:
My brother likes bananas, but they fill me with revulsion

And eating prunes or apples always gives me a convulsion

Brussels sprouts and cauliflowers just bring me out in spots

I'd advise you all to throw out every vegetable you've got

CHORUS AND KING:
You can't beat a muffin

There's absolutely nuffin

KING:
There's nuffin like a muffin every day.

CHORUS AND KING:
No you can't beat a muffin

There's absolutely nuffin

KING:
There's nuffin like a muffin every day.

One more time!

CHORUS AND KING:
You can't beat a muffin
There's absolutely nuffin

KING:
There's nuffin like a muffin every day.

The CHORUS dance off – but as they leave they turn back to the audience and as the music ends say
CHORUS:
There's absolutely nuffin!

HT: Well sung Sire!

KING: Yes – wasn't that jolly!

HT: I had a mule called Muffin you know. I called it Muffin the Mule.

KING: Fascinating. Fascinating. Who are you anyway?

HT: Cyril Sire. The Head Toadsman. Madly in love with your daughter Sire.

KING: Well that hardly narrows the field does it? Every young man I know is madly in love with my daughter…wotshername..

HT: Shirley Sire.

KING: Surely what?

HT: Shirley Sire. That's your daughter Sire. Princess Shirley.

KING: Is it? What about her?

HT: That's the one I'm madly in love with Sire.

KING: Ah yes – you were saying, weren't you? Well – good luck old boy! She's a looker – I'll give you that. But she's not an easy woman to please you know. Takes after her stepmother, the Queen. *(a loud angry cry of "HORACE!!" is heard from afar. It's THE QUEEN)*

KING: *(gloomily)* That's her now! Have you met?

HT: *(He's been an employee at the castle for several months; of course he's met her…)* Er..

KING: I wouldn't bother if I were you. Wish I hadn't…

PRINCESS AND THE TOAD 17

There's another loud angry cry of "HORACE!!" From slightly further away.

KING: *(ignoring her)* Anyway...about my daughter...

HT: Princess Shirley..

KING: That's the one.

HT: What about her Sire?

KING: I'm not averse to you marrying her Cecil.

HT: Cyril.

KING: What? No, no. Some mistake. My name's Horace. I'm sure it is.

HT: MY name's Cyril Sire.

KING: Really? How fascinating. Anyway, as I was saying...Cecil... I'm not averse to you marrying her. If she'll have you. But I need one thing in a son-in-law.

HT: What might that be Sire?

KING: Money.

HT: Money?

KING: And lots of it. Muffins don't come cheap you know... And you should see what the Queen spends on clothes and what-not.... Are you rich Cecil?

HT: Well not personally, Sire – but my father is very well off.

KING: Where did he get his money from?

HT: A bank Sire.

KING: A banker eh? Yes – they're all stinking rich.

HT: He didn't actually work in a bank Sire. He robbed one.

KING: Ah. Well. Shows a certain initiative I suppose.

HT: He's invested the money wisely Sire. So I should inherit a considerable fortune.

KING: Good. Good. I like the sound of that. You could be just the son-in-law I've been looking for. Tell me how are you getting on with Sheila..?

HT: Shirley.

KING: Whatever.

HT: Well everything was going swimmingly sir, until the arrival of the Royal Soothsayer with his ridiculous prophecy that the Princess would marry a toad.

KING: The man's an imbecile…

HT: You can say that again.

KING: The man's an imbecile. He only got the job because he's my brother.

HT: Spitting image of you Sire.

KING: Yes, well he's my twin isn't he? Goes with the territory.

HT: Of course.

KING: But tell the future? He can hardly tell the time of day. Who in their right mind could possibly believe that if you kiss enough toads one of them is going to turn into a handsome Prince?

HT: Exactly Sire!

KING: Exactly Sire. *(beat)* Frogs now – that's a different matter. One of my nephews was a frog you know. Spent the first years of his life living in a small pond on Wimbledon Common.

HT: You don't say so Sire?

KING: I do say so Sire. I just have done. But my point is that the Royal Soothsayer is losing his marbles if he thinks you can conjure a rich and handsome Prince from a mere toad. Never been done before; never will be done.

HT: I wish you'd tell your daughter that. Ever since the Royal Soothsayer came out with this toad malarkey, she's been down at the Royal Toadpool kissing them. Dropped me like a stone she did.

KING: Look upon it as a lucky escape, I would.

HT: But I love her Sire.

KING: Yes…Well we all have our crosses to bear –

(A scream – this time even angrier - of "HORACE!" From the not-yet-seen QUEEN)

KING: That's mine. I suppose I'd better see what the old bat wants. I've probably left the lid off the marmalade jar again.

HT: And I've got a fresh delivery of toads to deliver to the Royal Toadpool.

KING: Well then….thingy….we'd better leave these good people and go our respective ways. Toodlepip!

BLACKOUT AND MUSIC

SCENE 2 – THE ROYAL TOADPOOL

The curtain rises on the Royal Toadpool, where waits an enthusiastic PRINCESS SHIRLEY. The HEAD TOADSMAN enters with his large box marked "TOADS – THIS WAY UP" – only now he is carrying it upside down

HT: Fresh delivery of toads darling! *(He deposits a new batch of toads into the pool)*

PRINCESS: Do stop calling me darling!

HT: But you will always be my darling my dear. My very dear darling. My very dar dearling --

PRINCESS: You know perfectly well Cyril that our romance is at an end. I'm fond of you and all that, but I'm destined to marry a toad. It's been prophesied.

HT: It hurts me so much when you say that.

PRINCESS: You can't fight Fate you know. And it's so deliciously romantic to think that soon – very soon – I shall be betrothed to a handsome prince.

HT: Who was once a toad….

PRINCESS: Was does that matter?

HT: Well frankly I don't see anything romantic about marrying a warty old dry-skinned amphibian, who has spent most of his life wallowing in mud.

PRINCESS: You haven't got a romantic bone in your body, have you Cyril?

HT: I haven't got any warts either.

PRINCESS: Well my toad won't have warts . He'll no longer be a toad. He'll be a ravishingly attractive Prince – and he'll be all mine!

HT: I want to be all yours.

PRINCESS: Well you can't be. And that's that. And why are you still hanging around the palace anyway?

HT: To see you my darling. I took on the job of Head Toadsman just to be near you. Though every time you kiss a toad, every time you place your beautiful, red ruby lips on to a toad's repulsive little mouth, I feel like you're plunging a dagger into my very heart….

PRINCESS: Well you should grow up and get a life Cyril. I'm marrying a toad, whether you like it or not. Listen to this:

Music starts

Song: I'm Marrying a Toad

PRINCESS:
Every girl has a dream
Mine is not exactly what it seems
You may think that I'm deluded or mad
But I know what I know
And as prophecies go
It's neither unpleasant nor bad
For…
I'm marrying a toad

HT:
She's marrying a toad!

PRINCESS:
He'll turn into a Prince

HT:
He'll turn into a Prince

PRINCESS:
I'll give him a big kiss

HT:
She'll give him a big kiss

PRINCESS:
Which he wouldn't want to miss
'Cos I'm marrying a toad

HT:
She's marrying a toad

PRINCESS:
I'm not marrying a frog

HT:
She's not marrying a frog

PRINCESS:
Frogs are so passé

HT:
Frogs are so passé

PRINCESS:
My cousin was a frog
He was no use to man or dog
He's as lively as a log
I'm marrying a toad

PRINCESS:
Toads are clever, and they're cool
They don't just hang around the pool
Intelligent and fit
My toad will be a hit
He won't just be another froggy fool
I want you all to see

HT:
She wants us all to see

PRINCESS:
I'm glad as glad can be

HT:
She's glad as glad can be

PRINCESS:
I won't leave you in the dark
I'm happy as a lark

That I'm marrying a toad

HT:
She's marrying a toad

PRINCESS:
Yes - I'm marrying a toad

HT:
She's marrying a toad

PRINCESS:
Wow- I'm marrying a toad!

HT:
She's marrying a toad

PRINCESS:
Yes - I'm marrying a toad.

HT: *(sadly – spoken)* So you're marrying a toad then?

The ROYAL SOOTHSAYER rushes in. He looks astonishingly like the king, which is hardly surprising as he's a) the King's twin brother and b) played by the same actor..... A change of headgear is all that is required for him to change roles (as we shall see in the final scene) He has a broad Scottish accent.

ROYAL SOOTHSAYER: Ah – your Royal Highness. I'm so sorry I'm late. I got a bit lost in the Palace. I took the wrong turning. It's big isn't it?

PRINCESS: You came back from Glasgow five years ago Tiresias. You ought to be able to find your way around by now.

ROYAL SOOTHSAYER: I do apologise your majesty. Now – are we ready for the kissing ceremony to progress?

PRINCESS: *(enthusiastically)* I'm ready!

HT: I'm off

ROYAL SOOTHSAYER: Must you go so soon?

HT: *(going)* It's like a dagger in my heart watching all this you know. A dagger in my heart. *(He's gone)*

PRINCESS: Good riddance! I don't know what I ever saw in him. He's so wet you know.

ROYAL SOOTHSAYER: *(fishing a toad out of the pool)* These toads *(woof)* are rather wet I'm afraid, my Lady. But of course they would be, being submerged in water. Here's a new toad *(woof)*.

PRINCESS: Oh do stop barking!

ROYAL SOOTHSAYER: You know I can't help it your Royal Highness. Ever since your mother's sister– the Witch– put a curse on me, I'm unable to hear or say an animal's name without barking.

PRINCESS: Well it's extremely annoying for the rest of us.

ROYAL SOOTHSAYER: It's pretty annoying for me too.

PRINCESS: Let's get on with it, then…

ROYAL SOOTHSAYER: Do you know Your Royal Highness that toads *(woof)* are actually much more land-loving creatures than frogs *(woof.)* That's why toads *(woof)* have dry skin, while frogs *(woof)*, who of course spend most of their lives in water, are moist, and slimy. I don't know whether you've ever kissed a frog, *(woof)* your Royal Highness or even touched one, but you'll find that frogs *(woof)*–

PRINCESS: Oh do shut up Tiresias. I haven't come here for a natural history lesson – and nor have these good people. *(She waves distractedly at the audience)* We're here for the kissing bit. Hand me that toad!

ROYAL SOOTHSAYER: Woof. Very good my Lady. *(He does so)*

PRINCESS: *(She studies it eagerly)* Now Tiresias – tell me – will this be the one? Will this be my Prince Charming?

ROYAL SOOTHSAYER: I wouldn't know, your Royal Highness.

PRINCESS: But you're meant to know! You're paid to know! Knowing things is your job.

ROYAL SOOTHSAYER: *(gloomily)* I know.

PRINCESS: You look into the future and tell us what's going to happen. You're the Royal Soothsayer. You say sooths.…

PRINCESS AND THE TOAD

ROYAL SOOTHSAYER: Saying sooths is not the problem Princess. It's just that they're not always as...soothful...as you expect them to be.

PRINCESS: Well you better not have made a mistake with this prophecy. Right you warty little creature, let's be kissing you.

The ROYAL SOOTHSAYER obediently offers his cheek, but the PRINCESS instead plants a huge smacker on the toad's lips and waits for a reaction. There isn't any.....

PRINCESS: Nothing. No reaction whatsoever. He didn't even blink. *(She tosses him back angrily into the Royal Toadpool)*

ROYAL SOOTHSAYER: I'm sure he was overwhelmed to be favoured with your Royal lips my Lady.

PRINCESS: I'm not here, Tiresias, to brighten the lives of freshwater toads.

ROYAL SOOTHSAYER: Woof.

PRINCESS: I want a handsome prince and I want him sharpish! And if I don't get him soon, I'll fill this pool with piranha fish.

ROYAL SOOTHSAYER: Woof.

PRINCESS: And I'll make you their first meal.

ROYAL SOOTHSAYER: Ah. Right. Very good my lady!

PRINCESS: Now – be kind enough to fetch me another toad!

ROYAL SOOTHSAYER: *(sadly)* Woof.

BLACKOUT AND MUSIC

SCENE 3 – THE KING'S CHAMBER

We join the KING and his QUEEN in the middle of an argument – a not unusual state of affairs

QUEEN: And another thing Horace! How many times I have told you to put the loo seat down when you've finished in the lavatory.

KING: Oh I don't think that was me dear. Probably the Head Toadsman .. wotsisname

QUEEN: Don't be ridiculous! The Head Toadsman isn't allowed within a mile of the Royal Loo.

KING: He might have been caught short –

QUEEN: And why on earth you give him the run of the palace is beyond me.

KING: Well – I keep him on for old times' sake. His father was….you know……father to……him.

QUEEN: What?!

KING: Besides which he's stinking rich! The father. Made a fortune in…redistributing stuff…

The HEAD TOADSMAN shuffles in

HT: Beg pardon my Liege…

KING: Ah Cecil, we were just talking about you!

QUEEN: His name's Cyril you halfwit!

KING: Cyril? That's what I said wasn't it. *(He turns to audience for confirmation)* Wasn't it?

HT: Er –

KING: Anyway Squirrel – Cyril – what do you want?

HT: I just wanted to say – *(but he is interrupted by the arrival of PRINCESS SHIRLEY)*

PRINCESS: Mummy – have you see my jim-jams? Oh Cyril, you're still here. I thought you might have taken the hint by now.

HT: I could never leave you darling –

QUEEN: Darling!! Don't you darling my daughter. She's much too good for you. *(proudly)* She's going to marry a toad, you know.

PRINCESS AND THE TOAD

HT: Yes I did know actually.

QUEEN: Are you a toad?

HT: Er…no.

QUEEN: Ever been one?

HT: Well…no.

QUEEN: Any toads in the family?

HT: Not that I know of

QUEEN: He's an imposter Horace. Have his head cut off. Comes here pretending to be a toad!

HT: (*indignantly*) I'm not a toad!

QUEEN: (*triumphantly*) There we are! Condemned from his own mouth. *(shouts to someone offstage)* Take him away! Cut off his head! Next please!

PRINCESS: Mummy – that's a bit harsh isn't it? Cutting off his head.

QUEEN: You have to be cruel to be kind dear. And Stepmothers have a reputation to keep up. Horace – Escort him to the Royal Dungeons. We can't afford to pay for any more actors to play footmen.

HT: Look – I say!

QUEEN: That's quite enough from you Cyril.

PRINCESS: I'm sorry Cyril - but it's an awfully romantic way to die isn't it? Having your head cut off. All for the love of me.

HT: Er – yes, I suppose it is.

PRINCESS: Well be brave, won't you! I'll always keep a special spot in my heart just for you. Just here. *(She points to where she thinks her heart is)*

HT: Jolly good….

PRINCESS: And do let me know what time you're being executed, and I'll try and be there for you. Meantime I've got toads to kiss. See you later everybody! *(She skips off toward the Royal Toadpool)*

KING: Right then – well, look, sorry about this Cecil, but needs must when the devil drives eh?

QUEEN: What did you say, Horace?

KING: I wasn't referring to you my love. I was talking about…some other devil. Right then – thingy – let's wander down to the old dungeons shall we. I haven't been down there since…well last week actually.

HT: I don't want to inconvenience you Sire.

KING: No inconvenience at all old chap. I could do with a walk.

HT: Well then *(to THE QUEEN)* …goodbye your Majesty.

QUEEN: Goodbye Cyril. No hard feelings I hope. You might think me a little harsh, but Horace and I have standards to keep up. Unsuccessful suitors always lose their heads. It's a family tradition.

KING: *(going)* Maybe in your family my dear...

HT: Well I'm just wondering if -

QUEEN: It sounds cruel, I know. But as I said to my daughter – you have to be cruel to be kind. Cheerio!

THE KING and the HEAD TOADSMAN depart for the Royal Dungeons – but the actor playing the KING changes his headgear as he exits, and immediately makes an excited entrance followed shortly by the PRINCESS and the TOAD (played by the actor who was also the Head Toadsman.).

ROYAL SOOTHSAYER: *(out of breath and spluttering with excitement)* My Lords! My Laids! A moracle! A miracle! A mirvlous moracle!

QUEEN: What on earth are you burbling on about Horace?

ROYAL SOOTHSAYER: *(whispers)* Tiresias!

QUEEN: Eh?

ROYAL SOOTHSAYER: *(whispers)* I'm not Horace. I'm Tiresias, the Royal Soothsayer!

QUEEN: Of course you are. What on earth are you burbling on about Tiresias?

ROYAL SOOTHSAYER: You won't believe it Ma'am…

QUEEN: Try me

ROYAL SOOTHSAYER: In the Royal Tadpole Ma'am! – I mean the

PRINCESS AND THE TOAD

Royal Poadtool! There's been a miracle, a mirvlous moracle.

QUEEN: Calm down you stupid man and tell me in words of one syllable exactly what's happened.

ROYAL SOOTHSAYER: *(pulling himself together)* Well Ma'am – it's like this. I passed over a toad *(woof)* fresh from the pool, to your beautiful and gracious stepdaughter Princess Shirley –

QUEEN: Yes I know who my stepdaughter is, just get on with it man.

ROYAL SOOTHSAYER: Anyway, she placed her luscious lips upon the warty one's face, and lo and behold –

QUEEN: *(delighted)* He turned into a handsome Prince!

ROYAL SOOTHSAYER: He turned into a handsome Prince! And look – here he is Ma'am!

(And here he is indeed – entering, wearing a rather baffled look, followed by an ecstatic PRINCESS SHIRLEY)

PRINCESS: Oh Step-Mummy! I always knew it would work. Not bad looking is he?

QUEEN: *(admiringly)* He's fit!

TOAD: *(a bit embarrassed)* Nice to meet you

QUEEN: And he talks!

PRINCESS: Of course he talks! I'm not going to marry a mute, am I?

ROYAL SOOTHSAYER: *(to audience, as nobody is paying him the slightest bit of attention on stage)* First time I've been absolutely right about anything you know…

QUEEN: Hello handsome. I'm the Queen – Shirley's stepmother.

TOAD: You look awfully young to be a stepmother Ma'am.

QUEEN: I like this toad! What shall we call him?

PRINCESS: Prince Natterjack

QUEEN: Why Natterjack?

PRINCESS: A Natterjack is a particularly aristocratic sort of toad.

ROYAL SOOTHSAYER: Woof.

PRINCESS: It runs rather than hops and has a yellow stripe down his back.

ROYAL SOOTHSAYER: I wouldn't trust a fellow with a yellow stripe down his back, I can tell you.

PRINCESS: It's not there now you idiot!!

QUEEN: Have you looked darling?

PRINCESS: Well – no – I haven't actually looked ….yet ….

QUEEN: Do you have a yellow stripe down your back Natterjack?

TOAD: My name's actually Toby.

QUEEN/PRINCESS: *(both horrified)* Toby!

TOAD: Toby Toad.

ROYAL SOOTHSAYER: Woof.

PRINCESS: Don't be ridiculous – we can't call you Toby! I couldn't bear it.

ROYAL SOOTHSAYER: Woof.

PRINCESS: Whoever heard of a Prince Toby! No – you'll be Prince Natterjack from now on. And I shall be Princess Natterjack! Step-Mummy, I can hardly wait – can we get married this afternoon? Tiresias can do the ceremony.

QUEEN: Well I don't see why not dear. Your father would approve of a small private wedding. He's so mean with money.

PRINCESS: Brill!

QUEEN: We'll have to execute Cyril first though. It wouldn't be right for a failed suitor to still be alive when you married somebody else.

PRINCESS: Well that's OK – we can combine the two ceremonies. An execution followed by a marriage ceremony. Wot larks! That's probably never been done before.

ROYAL SOOTHSAYER: I wouldn't know.

QUEEN: Well that's settled then.

TOAD: Excuse me —

QUEEN: What is it?

TOAD: Do I have any say in this?

QUEEN: I'm afraid not Natterjack. You're marrying my daughter, and that's that. You're a very lucky man.

TOAD: But I'm a toad!

ROYAL SOOTHSAYER: Woof

PRINCESS: Not any more you're not. You're Prince Natterjack and I claim you for my lawful wedded husband.

TOAD: Ah.

QUEEN: Well come along darling! We've got to sort out your wedding dress. You can wear my old one. It's a bit frayed, but it'll be a perfect fit. If the moths haven't been at it…

ROYAL SOOTHSAYER: Woof!

PRINCESS: I'm so excited! Aren't you Natterjack!

TOAD: Er –

QUEEN: Come along darling! You'll have plenty of time to talk after you're married. Far too much time probably.

TOAD: Is there any –

QUEEN: As for you, Natterjack, you need a good shower. There's an unpleasant whiff of Royal Toadpool about you. Tiresias – there's an old suit of Horace's in that trunk he can wear. *(She waves at a conveniently placed trunk)*

ROYAL SOOTHSAYER: Yes Ma'am.

TOAD: I was wondering if –

PRINCESS: See you later darling! *(She kisses him on the cheek)* I'm sure he'll scrub up well Mummy.

(The QUEEN and her STEP-DAUGHTER exit, excitedly, leaving a bemused TOAD in the company of the ROYAL SOOTHSAYER)

ROYAL SOOTHSAYER: Well – aren't you a lucky young man then!

TOAD: I'm a toad!

ROYAL SOOTHSAYER: Woof.

TOAD: Excuse me asking, but were you once a dog?

ROYAL SOOTHSAYER: Woof. Whatever gave you that idea? No – nobody's ever kissed me and changed me into anything. Nobody's ever kissed me at all, come to think of it.

TOAD: Well I wish the Princess hadn't kissed me. I was very happy living as a toad.

ROYAL SOOTHSAYER: Woof.

TOAD: I had a beautiful wife and three lovely children. The eldest is about to sit his Toad-Levels. How on earth are they going to manage without me?

ROYAL SOOTHSAYER: Never mind you – what about me? I've spent years prophesying the Princess would marry this or that animal. Now that she's actually going to get married, I could be out of a job mate.

TOAD: That's a pity.

ROYAL SOOTHSAYER: Goodbye, good riddance, cheerio....Me with a wife and six little ones.

TOAD: Six little ones?

ROYAL SOOTHSAYER: Well actually no. No little ones. No wife either. It was poetic licence.

TOAD: I used to be very fond of poetry you know.

ROYAL SOOTHSAYER: You don't say? I thought you lot were all into fast cars and dramatic escapes from prison dressed as washerwomen. *(He is fiddling about with the trunk)*

TOAD: That was my cousin.

ROYAL SOOTHSAYER: Really. Nice bit of material this. *(He hands the toad a doublet)* Try it on.

TOAD: This is my favourite poem. Do you know it? *(He quotes earnestly and with deep feeling, while struggling at the same time to get into this ludicrously ill-fitting garment)*

See saw

Marjorie Daw

Johnny has got a new master.

He will get but a penny a day

(He lingers lovingly over this last line)

Because he can't work any faster.

Beautiful isn't it?

ROYAL SOOTHSAYER: I knew a Marjorie Daw once.

TOAD: Really?

ROYAL SOOTHSAYER: Or was it a Marion Daw?

TOAD: What wouldn't I give to be a toad again!

ROYAL SOOTHSAYER: Woof.

TOAD: I'm just not cut out to be a Prince. All that slaying dragons -

ROYAL SOOTHSAYER: Woof.

TOAD: -and rescuing maidens in distress malarkey. It's just not me.

ROYAL SOOTHSAYER: Can't say I'd fancy it either.

TOAD: I'd much rather curl up in the pool with a good Harry Potter book.

ROYAL SOOTHSAYER: Each to their own mate....

TOAD: And to be perfectly frank with you Mr Soothsayer, Princess Shirley seems a rather....forceful...sort of woman.

ROYAL SOOTHSAYER: Takes after her stepmother does our Shirl...

TOAD: Could you really see a marriage between the two of us working out?

ROYAL SOOTHSAYER: Search me mate. What do I know?

TOAD: I really don't think so....

ROYAL SOOTHSAYER: You could say ... *(He laughs delightedly at the thought)* you could say you're a toad *(woof)* in a hole!

TOAD: I couldn't have put it better myself!

Song: I'm a Toad in a Hole!

TOAD:
I'm a Toad...in a hole

Not a ferret or a badger or a vole
(ROYAL SOOTHSAYER woofs at each animal)

It was cool...in my pool

But now that I'm a Prince I feel a fool.

It was fun....in the sun

I was hopping round the lake with everyone

But now I'm here, I'll live in fear

Fighting battles, killing dragons every year

ROYAL SOOTHSAYER:
WOOF

TOAD:
As for Shirl, I feel a churl
But she's really not at all my kind of girl
Think of the strife, with her as my wife
And I've never killed a dragon in my life

ROYAL SOOTHSAYER:
WOOF

(These last lines sung very sadly and with feeling)

TOAD:
Can't you see
I want to be free
Simply me
I'm a Toad

ROYAL SOOTHSAYER:
WOOF

TOAD:
In a hole
I'm a Toad

ROYAL SOOTHSAYER: WOOF

TOAD:
Let me be

Let me be.

BLACKOUT AND MUSIC

SCENE 4 – THE PALACE RAMPARTS

There's a burst of theatrical lightening and a clap of thunder to mark the entrance of the WICKED WITCH – the final character in the play. She is clad, as befits a witch, entirely in black – black pointed hat, black cloak, black bag, broomstick – the lot. She is played by the actress who plays the Queen – but as the Queen is about to succumb to a sudden, rather unfortunate spell, this is not going to cause us any problems.

WITCH: Hello! Anybody there! I said anybody there!! *(She notices the audience, and looks at them disdainfully)* Oh so you are, are you? What an ugly lot ! This must be quite the ugliest audience I've ever seen. And I've seen a few ugly audiences. You should be ashamed of yourselves.

(She singles out a member of the audience)

Except for you little girl. You look quite attractive. Ever thought of being a witch? No?!! What's wrong with you? Don't you give me any cheek dearie, or I'll change you into a tuna fish sandwich! And don't you think I couldn't. Yesterday there was a little boy sitting just where you were, and he's now a sausage roll. Well he was a sausage roll. I ate him.

(reacts to audience)

Well I was hungry, wasn't I! You lose a lot of calories travelling around on one of these things

(She indicates her broomstick).

Why witches still have to use broomsticks, heaven alone knows. This is the twenty first century! We've invented the Apple iPad, the mobile phone, Bluetooth, Google Glasses, AI Chatbots – We can fly rockets to the moon - yet witches are still having to travel round on random bits of tree with twigs sticking out.

What was that? You don't believe I am a Witch!!! Right – you'll be chicken casserole before you can say abracadabra! I'll have you know that I am the Wicked Witch of the West! Well – the wicked Witch of the South West, if you're going to split hairs. Merton, Mitcham, Morden – that's my witchdom. I did once venture as far as Wimbledon Common Golf Club, but I'm not going there again.

(choose appropriate local place to denigrate)

Dreadful place. They've got plenty of witches of their own. I've got my own song you know. Would you like to hear it? Well too bad if you don't – I'm going to sing it anyway. Play my music minion!

Witch's Song

WITCH:
You don't get rich,
Being a witch….
But it's fun.
You don't get rich
Being a Witch.
For if I give my wand a twirl
I can turn you little girl
Into a scrumptious currant bun.
O yes I could – perhaps I should
Get on my broom
Fly round this room
And make a chicken casserole of
Everyone….

But don't despair.
I'm very fair
Ask anyone.
But don't despair.
I'm very fair
If you treat me with respect,
Admire my fearsome intellect,
Then we'll have fun.
In retrospect
We'll have a ball.
But if you make me hopping mad
I can be very, very bad
Turn your fingers into butter,

Throw your toys into the gutter,
Every one…

Every Witch
Must have a cat
I can't stand mine.
For every witch must have a cat
My cat is called Matilda
Several times I've nearly killed her
But then again, a cat has got nine lives.
She is lazy and pernicious
And occasionally vicious
A crazy mixed-up mog
Who thinks she is a dog
Can you believe it?

But I'm so glad
That I'm so bad
It's a laugh.
Yes, I'm so glad
That I'm bad.
I gave myself three wishes
Never wash or dry the dishes
I never floss between my teeth
Nor have a bath.
My bedroom's a disgrace
Looks like someone's trashed the place,
But nothing goes to waste
Cos my magic spells are ace!
Yes, I'm a witch! A lovely witch!
Yes, I'm a witch! I'm a witch, I'm a wi…..tch. I'm a witch!

WITCH: Wasn't that brilliant! Now listen, I'm looking for my godson, Cyril. His mother's very worried about him. He's fallen in love with some daffy Princess apparently and hasn't been home now for six months. Any of you seen him? Come on – answer me – answer me - or you'll all be chocolate mousse before we finish this play! He's where? He's where? Behind me?! I've never heard anything so ridiculous. This isn't a pantomime! What do you take me for? Some sort of idiot?

But CYRIL is indeed behind her. He's been led onto stage by the ROYAL SOOTHSAYER, who is carrying a large axe. CYRIL is in handcuffs.

HT: Auntie Bertha!

WITCH: Hello Cyril dear. Why are you wearing handcuffs? Is that some sort of fashion accessory? I know what you young people are like.

ROYAL SOOTHSAYER: You two know each other?

WITCH: Of course we know each other. Cyril is my godson. Not a particularly creditable one, but one can't be responsible for one's relatives. Now get me King Horace immediately.

ROYAL SOOTHSAYER: I'm afraid his Majesty is engaged on highly important affairs of state just at present. *(He can't resist it)* A small matter of a prophecy of mine being fulfilled. Not for the first time, I might add…

WITCH: How long's he going to be? *(She indicates the broomstick)* I'm on a flying visit.

ROYAL SOOTHSAYER: He certainly won't be available to see you today.

WITCH: I beg your pardon? Do you know who I am?

ROYAL SOOTHSAYER: You're his Auntie Bertha

WITCH: I'm a witch!

ROYAL SOOTHSAYER: Which what?

WITCH: Do you want me to turn you into a microwave oven?

ROYAL SOOTHSAYER: You mean you do spells and that?

WITCH: Of course

ROYAL SOOTHSAYER: Then how do you spell blancmange? *(He laughs, delighted by his own joke.)*

WITCH: *(turns to a member of the audience)* Are you laughing at me sonny? Go on then – you spell blancmange! You can't can you? Look it up in the dictionary when you get home, or I'll turn you into a lemon meringue pie. And I bet you can't spell meringue either. You see I'm not some feeble do-gooder wizard, who's been to Hogwarts, and just wants to make the world a better place. I'm a fully-fledged, card-carrying witch!

HT: Yes…a word of advice young fella…I wouldn't get on the wrong side of Auntie Bertha. Her bite is worse than her bark. She turned my best friend into a beetle.

ROYAL SOOTHSAYER: Woof.

WITCH: Hold on a moment – I know you don't I? We met at Horace's second wedding. You're the idiot who brought me a glass of tepid white wine when I asked for a Vodka Martini!

ROYAL SOOTHSAYER: *(horrified)* You're the one who put that curse on me!

WITCH: The very same sweetheart! How's it working? Cyril – let's have a song and find out shall we?

HT: Er…Well I'm not really in much of a singing mood Auntie

WITCH: Oh don't be such a wet blanket Cyril. Count your blessings I always say. You must have something to be glad about.

HT: *(defiantly)* Well I'm glad I'm not a toad, I'll tell you that.

ROYAL SOOTHSAYER: Woof.

WITCH: That'll do nicely! Fill your song with animals Cyril and we'll have a bit of fun. Play some music!

Song: - "I'm Glad I'm Not a Toad"

HT:
I'm glad I'm not a mole

SOOTHSAYER:
Woof!

HT:
And I'm glad I'm not a vole

SOOTHSAYER:
Woof!

HT:
I'm glad I'm not a ram

SOOTHSAYER:
Woof!

HT:
And I'm glad I'm not a lamb

SOOTHSAYER:
Woof!

HT:
I'm glad I'm not a goat

SOOTHSAYER:
Woof!

HT:
And I'm glad I'm not a stoat

SOOTHSAYER:
Woof!

HT:
But I really would explode

If I had to be a toad!

SOOTHSAYER:
Woof!

The SOOTHSAYER is beginning to enjoy this now. His "woofs" become more frenetic as the song proceeds

HT:
I'm glad I'm not a wren

SOOTHSAYER:
Woof!

HT:
And I'm glad I'm not a hen

SOOTHSAYER:
Woof!

HT:
I'm glad I'm not a hare

SOOTHSAYER:
Woof

HT:
And I'm glad I'm not a …….

(He pauses – and turns to the audience)
Help! Think of an animal that rhymes with "hare" ….

(A call of "bear" is made – if not from the audience, then from backstage)

HT:
I'm glad I'm not a bear

SOOTHSAYER:
Woof!

HT:
I'm glad I'm not a stork

SOOTHSAYER:
Woof!

HT:
And I'm glad I'm not a hawk

SOOTHSAYER:
Woof!

HT:
But I really would explode

If I had to be a toad!

SOOTHSAYER:
Woof!

SOOTHSAYER:
Help me with the "woofs" everybody!

HT:
Oh I'm so glad I'm not a mouse

SOOTHSAYER AND ALL :
Woof!

HT:
And I'm glad I'm not a louse

SOOTHSAYER AND ALL :
Woof!

HT:
I'm glad I'm not a bird

SOOTHSAYER AND ALL :
Woof!

HT:
For that would be absurd!

(The SOOTHSAYER – appalled that he has no opportunity for a "woof" looks at him reproachfully; HT reproaches those in the audience who have woofed!)

HT:
For I cannot even fly

SOOTHSAYER AND ALL :
Woof!

HT:
As I'm not a butterfly

SOOTHSAYER AND ALL :
Woof!

HT:
But I really would explode

If I had to be a toad.

SOOTHSAYER AND ALL :
Woof!

Other cast members come in as chorus for this final verse

HT:
I'm glad I'm not a flea

SOOTHSAYER AND ALL :
Woof!

CHORUS:
He's so glad he's not a flea

SOOTHSAYER AND ALL :
Woof!

HT:
And I'm glad I'm not a bee

SOOTHSAYER AND ALL :
Woof!

CHORUS:
He's so glad he's not a bee

SOOTHSAYER AND ALL :
Woof!

HT:
I'm glad I'm not a shark

SOOTHSAYER AND ALL:
Woof!

CHORUS:
He's so glad he's not a shark

SOOTHSAYER AND ALL:
Woof!

HT:
Or a dog who always barks

SOOTHSAYER AND ALL:
Woof!

CHORUS:
Or a dog who always barks

SOOTHSAYER AND ALL:
Woof!

HT:
I'm so glad I'm not a cat

SOOTHSAYER AND ALL:
Woof!

HT:
And I'm glad I'm not a bat

SOOTHSAYER AND ALL:
Woof!

HT:
I'm so glad I'm not a gnat

SOOTHSAYER AND ALL:
Woof!

HT:
And I'm glad I'm not a sprat

SOOTHSAYER AND ALL:
Woof!

> **HT:**
> I'm glad I'm not a rat
>
> **SOOTHSAYER AND ALL:**
> Woof!
>
> **CHORUS:**
> He's glad he's not a rat
>
> **SOOTHSAYER AND ALL:**
> Woof!
>
> **HT AND CHORUS:**
> I'm /He's just as glad as glad can be
> And it's very very plain to see
> It's what all of us have knowed
> I'm/He's so glad I'm/He's not a toad *(Woof!)*
>
> **SOOTHSAYER AND CHORUS:**
> He's so glad he's not a toad *(Woof!)*
>
> **HT:**
> I'm so glad I'm not a toad *(Woof!)*
>
> **SOOTHSAYER AND CHORUS:**
> He's so glad he's not a to…..ad *(Woof!)*
>
> **HT:**
> I'm so glad I'm not a toad.... *(Woof!)*

WITCH: Right – Well sung both of you! What a pair of woofers you are! Now I need a few private words with my godson. Off you go Tiresias.

ROYAL SOOTHSAYER: I'm afraid I'm not at liberty to leave you alone with this person Ma'am. As it happens we're on our way to -

But he never finishes his sentence as the WITCH unleashes a torrent of animals at him, to which the poor old SOOTHSAYER can only respond with ever-increasingly desperate "woofs", eventually he rushes off stage to get away from this appalling woman…

WITCH: Dog! Cat! Mouse! Rat! Ferret! Mongoose! Tiger! Lion! Octopus! Crocodile! Barbary Ape! Proboscis Monkey!

Tyrannosaurus! *(SOOTHSAYER has left by now. Woofing pathetically)* Mmm...one of my more successful curses I'd say Cyril. So how are you dear? You're looking a bit peeky.

HT: Well I was just on my way to have my head cut off Auntie.

WITCH: Really? I wouldn't advise doing that if I were you. Your mother won't like it

HT: I'm not sure I would either.

WITCH: Mind you, some of my best friends don't have heads.

HT: Auntie, I don't want to have my head cut off. It's just that King Horace has insisted I must. Well – actually it's not so much him as the Queen.

WITCH: Beatrice! A dreadful woman! Dreadful woman! A mild curse should sort her out. (S*he pulls out her wand and mutters an incantation. There's another flash of lightening.*) There – that should do it Cyril. I've confined her to bed for the foreseeable future. She'll be stuck between the sheets until I release her. And you can be quite sure she'd never sanction an execution without being there to watch it. She likes to be the centre of attention.

HT: *(deeply relieved)* You're a brick Auntie Bertha. How will I ever be able to thank you!

WITCH: My pleasure dear. Now then I must fly. Is there anything else I can do for you before I go?

HT: *(sadly)* Nobody can help me Auntie. I'm in love with Princess Shirley, but she's set her heart on marrying a toad..

WITCH: Surely you mean a frog?

HT: No, no – It's definitely a toad.

WITCH: Well there's no accounting for taste I suppose.. When is she proposing to marry this toad?

HT: At the Royal Toadpool in half an hour. Shortly after I've been executed.

WITCH: Well we'll see about that, won't we? Oh and Cyril –

HT: Yeah?

WITCH: Do take those ridiculous handcuffs off will you. This isn't Fifty Shades of Grey. We wouldn't want to give Princess Shirley the wrong idea about you, would we?

BLACKOUT & MUSIC

SCENE 5 – THE ROYAL TOADPOOL

Enter the KING, the PRINCESS (in full bridal regalia) and the TOAD (looking ridiculous in one of the king's cast-off suits)

KING: Right then Crackerjack –

PRINCESS: Natterjack Daddy!

KING: Same thing, same thing! "A rose by any other name would smell as sweet" as er….Shakesdagger once said. Now – where's your stepmother?

PRINCESS: She's fast asleep Daddy! I can't wake her up!

KING: *(not entirely displeased to hear this news)* Ah well. These things happen. Probably some sort of curse I expect. We'll get this Toad Prince to kiss her sometime. That might do the trick.

PRINCESS: Will we have to postpone the wedding Daddy?

TOAD: I wouldn't mind – *(but nobody is paying any attention to him)*

KING: I don't see why do you? I'm sure your stepmother would want the show to go on. She's a great trooper Belinda.

PRINCESS: Beatrice.

KING: Whatever.

TOAD: Excuse me… I –

KING: Who the hell are you?

TOAD: I'm the toad, Sire.

KING: Course you are, course you are. I knew that Bacharach… No need to tell me! You're the groom, aren't you? Lucky man! Now all we need now is my brother, the Royal Soothsayer to perform the marriage ceremony.

PRINCESS: He's probably got lost again Daddy. He's hopeless. He's always getting lost in the palace.

There's a pause – while they all look at each other. Slowly they realise what the audience have realised some time ago…. For a moment they come out of character

KING: Er…are you thinking what I'm thinking?

PRINCESS: No budget left for a fifth actor….?

TOAD: That's why you're the "spitting image" of your brother……

KING: Oh well – needs must I suppose.

(He rushes out, grabs the Royal Soothsayer's cap and re-enters immediately as the Royal Soothsayer. From now on much of the fun in this scene comes from him having to switch rapidly from character to character, by the uncomplicated process of wearing a crown for the King and a flat cap for the Soothsayer....)

ROYAL SOOTHSAYER: I do apologise your Royal Highness. I got a little lost on my way down here. I found myself in the Royal Loo and I couldn't get out.

KING: *(who moves rapidly to his throne, every time he speaks)* Did you put the seat down?

ROYAL SOOTHSAYER: *(rushing back to a standing position – and so on throughout the scene)* I always put the seat down Sire.

KING: Right – well let's get on with it then.

ROYAL SOOTHSAYER: But where is Her Majesty, Your Majesty?

KING: Er.. She's having a bit of a lie-in. I shouldn't have to tell you this brother.. Honestly, what's the point of employing someone to tell us what's what if he doesn't know who's where?

PRINCESS: Stop blathering Daddy! I can't wait to get married…

KING: Fair enough darling. There's just the small matter of the "financial settlement" that we need to talk about. *(to the TOAD)* I take it that you're not short of a bob or two eh Haversack?

TOAD: I don't have a penny to my name Sire.

KING: *(appalled)* What?!

PRINCESS: Of course he doesn't have a penny to his name Daddy! He's a toad!

ROYAL SOOTHSAYER: Woof.

KING: Well that rather complicates matters –

PRINCESS: No it doesn't Daddy! Not in the slightest. That's what so wonderfully romantic about all this! Think about it - a penniless animal turned into a handsome Prince. What more could you want?

KING: Money for starters….

PRINCESS: Oh Daddy, don't be so mercenary! Mummy's quite right about you. It's always money, money, money where you're concerned. Aren't there rather more important things. Like romance? Like passion? Like love?

TOAD: If I could just point out –

KING AND PRINCESS: Oh do be quiet!

TOAD: It's just that I don't really want to get married Sire.

KING: Well that's extremely ill-mannered of you Haversack. Many a young man has lost his head over my daughter.

TOAD: I can well believe that.

KING: Cecil for one! Did you dispatch him as I commanded Tiresias?

ROYAL SOOTHSAYER: Well I was going to talk to you about Sire. You see –

KING: *(not listening)* Good, good. Though a shame really – I quite liked the fella. He had a muffin called Mule you know.

PRINCESS: Daddy!

KING: All right darling! You've convinced me. Brother– let the service begin!

ROYAL SOOTHSAYER: Very well my Liege. *(to nobody in particular offstage)* Sound the fanfare! *(a fanfare sounds – then as if in a boxing ring, he announces the two participants)*

In the left-hand corner, the beautiful thrice-married, thrice-widowed daughter of King Horace and Queen Beatrice. That glowing, glamorous, glittering slip of a girl, admired by all, and married to some, I give you – and you can have her– Princess Shirley!!!

PRINCESS SHIRLEY simpers and pouts as from offstage comes the sound of rapturous applause that ends almost as soon as it has begun.

In the right-hand corner, the envy of all, once a common or garden freshwater Toad (woof) now elevated to the highest honour in Southwest London, and to riches and renown beyond his wildest dreams – let's hear it for… The Toad! Woof.

The same sudden burst of applause, which cuts out equally abruptly.

TOAD: *(sadly)* I just want to be a toad again….

PRINCESS AND THE TOAD

ROYAL SOOTHSAYER: Woof

KING: *(kindly)* Wedding nerves old boy. We all have them. Bear up!

ROYAL SOOTHSAYER: Woof!

KING: Be a man!

TOAD: But I'm a -

ROYAL SOOTHSAYER: Right then. I'll keep it fairly short. Do you Princess Shirley take this toad *(woof)* to be your lawful wedded husband?

PRINCESS: *(in seventh heaven)* I do!!

ROYAL SOOTHSAYER: Do you – you...animal you... take Princess Shirley as your lawful wedded wife.

TOAD: Well - I suppose if I -

There's a sudden flash of lightening again and – yes – we all know who's suddenly turned up....

WITCH: Stop the ceremony! There's been a mistake!

Consternation all round

KING: Bertha! *(they evidently know each other – the King even remembers her name)* What on earth are you doing here?

WITCH: I've come to stop your daughter from making a terrible mistake!

PRINCESS: What do you mean?

WITCH: I regret to say this toad's a fraud.

ROYAL SOOTHSAYER: Woof.

PRINCESS: A fraud!

KING: I say!

WITCH: He's not a toad at all.

ROYAL SOOTHSAYER: Woof

TOAD: I am a toad.

ROYAL SOOTHSAYER: Woof.

WITCH: Oh woof off! *(There's another lightening flash)* There! I've removed the curse I put on you. Now keep your mouth shut.

ROYAL SOOTHSAYER: Oh – thanks very much!

PRINCESS: Look– I don't know who you are, and I don't care – but I'm telling you this man is a toad!

(*The ROYAL SOOTHSAYER is on the point of barking – and then, to his delight, realises he doesn't have to…*)

WITCH: No he isn't.

PRINCESS: He is a toad. I kissed him didn't I? I should know.

WITCH: That's as maybe.

KING: Are you a toad Crackerjack?

PRINCESS: Of course he's a toad. Daddy. I saw him, I tell you. He had a yellow stripe down his back.

KING: *(meaningfully)* Had he by Jove!

TOAD: I really don't -

WITCH: A trick of the light my dear. I'm afraid. This said toad is nothing but a jumped-up frog!

KING/PRINCESS/TOAD: A Frog!!

WITCH: *(to HORACE)* As such, of course, he's quite unworthy of your daughter's hand Horace, as I'm sure you'll agree.

KING: Absolutely. Your prophecy definitely said "toad" didn't it Ty?

ROYAL SOOTHSAYER: It certainly did.

KING: There we are then!

PRINCESS: *(desperate)* Look you can't prove he was a frog!

WITCH: Oh yes I can!

PRINCESS: Oh no you can't!

WITCH: Oh yes I can!

TOAD: You can prove I'm not a toad madam?

WITCH: No problem at all.

PRINCESS: How?

WITCH: By reversing the enchantment of course.

KING: *(penny dropping)* You mean you can turn him into whatever he was, before he turned into whatever he is?

WITCH: Admirably put Horace.

PRINCESS: I haven't the faintest idea what you're talking about

WITCH: A simple spell, my dear, will prove once and for all what this creature was before having the misfortune to come into contact with your ruby red lips.

KING: Splendid! Splendid! I enjoy a good spell. You've no objections I take it Tog – Froad – whatever you are?

TOAD: *(seeing light at the end of the tunnel)* Only too pleased to be of service Your Majesty.

KING: Good, good. Most sporting of you. Right – over to you Bertha.

WITCH: *(authoritative)* Right then Frog – stand in the pool over there will you. *(the pool is off-set, and can't be seen by the audience)*

PRINCESS: But he'll get his clothes all wet!

WITCH: He won't be needing clothes again dear. *(She turns to front row of audience)* Now you lot – sit right back in your seats, or you'll all be turned into frogs. And we wouldn't want that would we?

KING: *(to nobody in particular – as an actor)* Are we insured for that?

WITCH: Quiet – all of you! Dim the lights! *(they dim...)* Now then. *(She takes out her wand, and proceeds to chant, in utter seriousness)*

Be you frog, or be you toad

Turn into your former mode!

There's a bang, a flash, and when the lights come back on, there's no sign of the man. The PRINCESS rushes to the pool, and triumphantly brings back a toad.

PRINCESS: There! What did I tell you! He's a toad *(She chucks him at her father)*

KING: Looks like a toad to me Bertha. Warts and all! *(Se chucks the toad back to his daughter)*

PRINCESS: And there's a yellow stripe down his back! *(She chucks him to the Witch)*

WITCH: *(totally unworried)* So there is! Yes – no doubt about it. He's a toad all right. Sorry – I must have mistaken him for somebody else. *(she chucks the toad back to the Princess)*

PRINCESS: Well – change him back into a Prince again.

WITCH: Oh no – I can't do that. My spells only work one-way.

PRINCESS: What?!

WITCH: It's annoying, but there you are.

PRINCESS: You mean to say you knew when you changed him into a toad, that you couldn't change him back.

WITCH: Why yes of course.

KING: Why didn't you say?

WITCH: You never asked. I'm not a mind-reader Horace.

PRINCESS: But that's outrageous!

WITCH: It's a little awkward!

KING: Try kissing him again dear.

WITCH: Oh no that won't do any good. These kissing spells only work once you know. Kissing's never the same the second time round.

And the lack of success that greets THE PRINCESS'S frantic kisses prove her point.

PRINCESS: She's right!

WITCH: Of course I'm right. I'm always right.

KING: *(dubiously)* Ye..es

ROYAL SOOTHSAYER: Shall I proceed with the marriage service Your Majesty?

PRINCESS: Don't be ridiculous! I'm not marrying a toad!

ROYAL SOOTHSAYER: Well I can't stop the service halfway through Sire. It would be most irregular.

PRINCESS: I never want to see another toad again in my life. *(She chucks her betrothed at the Royal Soothsayer)* Tiresias. Take this wretched animal and chuck him back in the pond where he came from.

ROYAL SOOTHSAYER: But the service your Majesty…..

WITCH: Well I might be able to help you on this one sweeties. I happen to know my godson is very taken with the Princess.

Though I can't for the life of me think why.

KING: Is he rich?

PRINCESS: Is he fit?

WITCH: Well you can ask him yourselves. He just happens to be waiting in the foyer. *(calling off)* Cyril! This is your cue.

HT: *(emerging from the opposite side to the toad's exit)* Hello darling!

PRINCESS: Cyril!

HT: My dearest darling, my very dar dearling…

KING: Cecil! Why, what a surprise. I thought you were dead!

HT: Well I promise you I'm not Sire

KING: Excellent! How's your father?

HT: *(surprised)* He was all right when I last saw him My Liege

WITCH: Cyril was hoping he might be of some service to you both.

KING: Really – how?

HT: I was wondering if I might have the great good fortune of marrying your daughter Sire. It seems a shame to stop the service just because of the unfortunate disappearance of the groom.

KING: Well I don't see why not.

ROYAL SOOTHSAYER: But a marriage not to a toad would ruin my reputation Sire.

KING: I very much doubt it brother. Shelley – what do you think?

PRINCESS: *(annoyed)* Sheila!

KING: Well what does she think?

WITCH: I'd just like to add - and I don't know if this will make any difference to her decision - but if your daughter does not take up my godson's kind offer, I shall have no alternative but to turn her into a bacon butty.

BEAT

KING: Well I think that's a bit of a clincher old girl, don't you?

PRINCESS: *(doubtfully)* Well I suppose I could do worse. I was once very fond of Cyril.

KING: That's the spirit! And he's got pots of money you know! At least his father has. Where is he now Cedric?

HT: In prison sir.

KING: Ah well – he'll be out soon I expect eh? Right – get on with it thingy.

ROYAL SOOTHSAYER: *(somewhat flustered)* Yes. Where was I? Er…do you your Toadship – that is to say Cyril, formerly Head Toadsman, take Princess Shirley here for your lawful wedded wife?

HT: *(overjoyed)* I most certainly do!

ROYAL SOOTHSAYER: *(to PRINCESS)* What about you?

PRINCESS: *(sulkily)* S'pose so.

ROYAL SOOTHSAYER: Excellent. I now pronounce you man and wife. Cyril – you may kiss the bride.

KING: Careful she doesn't turn into a toad Squirrel!

WITCH: *(confidentially to HORACE as the newly-weds smooch)* There's plenty of time for that to happen Horace.

KING: Ah Bertha – seeing you today - brings back of lot of memories you know!

WITCH: Yes – for me too Horace! I did warn you about Beatrice didn't I?

KING: I suppose it was you who put her under this sleeping spell?

WITCH: Indeed it was. But of course I'll release her whenever you say.

KING: *(reflectively)* Ye…es. Well - there's no hurry is there. A few days in bed will do wonders for the old girl. *(They smile conspiratorially)*

HT: *(approaches)* My liege – Auntie Bertha –I just want to say that this is the happiest day of my life!

KING: Jolly good! Jolly good. Just as well you weren't executed eh! But we must all count our blessings! Let's sing your jolly toad song again shall we Cyril? Give the audience their money's worth.

(A song sheet drops down so the audience can join in)

HT: And let's pretend we've all been cursed by the Witch .

KING: Why on earth do that?

HT: That way we can all join in the Woofs! *(music)* Right then - All together now!

Song: - "I'm Glad I'm Not a Toad!

HT:
I'm glad I'm not a mole

SOOTHSAYER AND ALL :
Woof!

HT:
And I'm glad I'm not a vole

SOOTHSAYER AND ALL :
Woof!

HT:
I'm glad I'm not a ram

SOOTHSAYER AND ALL :
Woof!

HT:
And I'm glad I'm not a lamb

SOOTHSAYER AND ALL :
Woof!

HT:
I'm glad I'm not a goat

SOOTHSAYER AND ALL :
Woof!

HT:
And I'm glad I'm not a stoat

SOOTHSAYER AND ALL :
Woof!

HT:
But I really would explode
If I had to be a toad!

SOOTHSAYER AND ALL :
Woof!

HT:
I'm glad I'm not a wren

SOOTHSAYER AND ALL :
Woof!

HT:
And I'm glad I'm not a hen

SOOTHSAYER AND ALL :
Woof!

HT:
I'm glad I'm not a hare

SOOTHSAYER AND ALL :
Woof!

HT:
And I'm glad I'm not a bear

SOOTHSAYER AND ALL :
Woof!

HT:
I'm glad I'm not a stork

SOOTHSAYER AND ALL :
Woof!

HT:
And I'm glad I'm not a hawk

SOOTHSAYER AND ALL :
Woof!

HT:
But I really would explode

If I had to be a toad!

SOOTHSAYER AND ALL :
Woof!

HT:
Oh I'm so glad I'm not a mouse

SOOTHSAYER AND ALL :
Woof!

HT:
And I'm glad I'm not a louse

SOOTHSAYER AND ALL :
Woof!

HT:
I'm glad I'm not a bird

SOOTHSAYER AND ALL :
Woof!

HT:
For that would be absurd!

For I cannot even fly

SOOTHSAYER AND ALL :
Woof!

HT:
As I'm not a butterfly

SOOTHSAYER AND ALL :
Woof!

HT:
But I really would explode

If I had to be a toad.

SOOTHSAYER AND ALL :
Woof!

Other cast members come in as chorus for this final verse

HT:
I'm glad I'm not a flea

SOOTHSAYER AND ALL :
Woof!

CHORUS:
He's so glad he's not a flea

SOOTHSAYER AND ALL :
Woof!

HT:
And I'm glad I'm not a bee

SOOTHSAYER AND ALL :
Woof!

CHORUS:
He's so glad he's not a bee

SOOTHSAYER AND ALL :
Woof!

HT:
I'm glad I'm not a shark

SOOTHSAYER AND ALL:
Woof!

CHORUS:
He's so glad he's not a shark

SOOTHSAYER AND ALL:
Woof!

HT:
Or a dog who always barks

SOOTHSAYER AND ALL:
Woof!

CHORUS:
Or a dog who always barks

SOOTHSAYER AND ALL:
Woof!

HT:
I'm so glad I'm not a cat

SOOTHSAYER AND ALL:
Woof!

HT:
And I'm glad I'm not a bat

SOOTHSAYER AND ALL:
Woof!

HT:
I'm so glad I'm not a gnat

SOOTHSAYER AND ALL:
Woof!

HT:
And I'm glad I'm not a sprat

SOOTHSAYER AND ALL:
Woof!

HT:
I'm glad I'm not a rat

SOOTHSAYER AND ALL:
Woof!

CHORUS:
He's glad he's not a rat

SOOTHSAYER AND ALL:
Woof!

HT AND CHORUS:
I'm /He's just as glad as glad can be
And it's very plain to see
It's what all of us have knowed
I'm/He's so glad I'm/He's not a toad *(Woof!)*

SOOTHSAYER AND CHORUS:
He's so glad he's not a toad *(Woof!)*

HT:
I'm so glad I'm not a toad *(Woof!)*

SOOTHSAYER AND CHORUS:
He's so glad he's not a to…..ad *(Woof!)*

HT:
I'm so glad I'm not a toad…. *(Woof!)*

KING: *(to audience)* That's it everybody! But do come again. Bring some friends. Frogs and Toads get in for half price – parents pay top whack! And remember as you go out – a word of advice from someone who knows a bit about life. Never kiss a toad if you can help it!

CURTAIN

BEAST

First performance at Colour House Theatre, Easter 2018

ORIGINAL CAST:
KING HORACE/ROYAL SOOTHSAYER: Neil Summerville
QUEEN BEATRICE/WITCH: Sophia Lorenti
RAPUNZEL: Abbie Andrews
JACK/BEAST: Will Howard
INTRODUCTION (RECORDED VOICE): Judi Dench

SCENES

SCENE 1 - The Royal Throne Room
SCENE 2 - The Wild Wood
SCENE 3 - The Beast's Parlour
SCENE 4 - The Wild Wood
SCENE 5 - The Beast's Drawing Room

BEAST

INTRODUCTION (*Originally recorded by Judi Dench – can be cut*)

Hello and welcome to *[insert theatre name]*

My name's *[insert name]* and I'm very interested in trees.

Now – just a few housekeeping notices before we start the play.

In case there's a fire – and there won't be - please exit calmly and quietly either from the way you've just come in.... Or from the exit that the tall, bald man is pointing at now.

And please make sure you turn off your mobile phones.

We have a Witch in the cast who has a nasty habit of turning the owners of mobile phones that ring into tuna fish sandwiches. And we wouldn't want that, would we?

Right settle down everyone, and enjoy the show.

And don't be frightened by the Beast! I've kissed a few beasts in my time and believe me, their barks are always worse than their bites.

Ladies and Gentlemen, boys and girls....we present BEAST!

SCENE 1 – THE ROYAL THRONE ROOM

The curtain opens to reveal KING HORACE, crown askew and legs dangling over an easy chair, munching his way through a rapidly diminishing pile of muffins. His face is streaked with butter and his shirt sleeves covered in jam. He seems surprised but unconcerned to find himself the centre of attention

KING: (*noticing the audience*) Ah – hello. Just having a muffin. You can't beat them. Some people prefer toasted teacakes of course – or hot buttered scones dripping with honey - but I've always been a muffin-man myself.

Fancy one little girl ? You do? Well sorry about that. I'm afraid there are none left! *(and indeed there aren't; the King has just shoved the last one into his mouth.)* Another time perhaps...

He is interrupted by a cry of "HORACE" from offstage. The King curls up on his throne and makes urgent sshing motions to audience.

QUEEN: (*entering calling loudly*) Horace!!! *Horace*!!!

KING: (*almost choking on muffin*) Ah darling, there you are! I've been looking for you everywhere.

QUEEN: (*sarcastic*) Well I suggest you try the Royal Throne Room.

KING: (*getting off throne*) Excellent idea! I'll go and have a look there now.

QUEEN: This *is* the Royal Throne Room, you dunderhead. And I'm *here* aren't I?

KING: Ah yes, so you are. Well found! That was clever of me.

QUEEN: You're an impossible human being Horace! I don't know what on earth possessed me to marry you.

KING: Probably the fact that I'm the King I expect.

QUEEN: Well it certainly wasn't for your stunning good looks.

KING: No – that was my point actually. It was more the money, the power and the status I have as King. I find – generally speaking of course – that those are the principal things that make me attractive to women.

QUEEN: Stop wittering on Horace. I want to talk to you about Rapunzel.

KING: Ah. Jolly good. Rapunzel eh?

QUEEN: Yes.

KING: And….er…who exactly *is* Rapunzel?

QUEEN: Your daughter? My stepdaughter?

KING: I thought that was Sheila…Shelley….Shirley….

QUEEN: Your *younger* daughter Horace

KING: Ah yes, of course. My *younger* daughter! It had quite slipped my mind that I *had* a younger daughter.

QUEEN: Well what are we going to do with her?

KING: What am I going to do with her?

QUEEN: Yes

KING: Er…what exactly had you in mind?

QUEEN: The prophecy Horace…..

KING: What prophecy might that be my dear?

QUEEN: From Tiresias – your twin brother?

KING: I thought I was an only twin.

QUEEN: That she would marry the Beast?

KING: The Beast? That sounds a bit drastic. Which beast were you thinking of?

QUEEN: Oh Horace! Sometimes I Just despair of you. Would it help if I put it all into a song?

KING: Oh yes dear. I love a good song! And I wondered what that music was. *(for music has started playing)*

Song: Your Daughter is Marrying The Beast

QUEEN:
Your daughter is marrying the Beast

KING:
The Beast?

QUEEN:
Soon we'll have the wedding feast

KING:
(*pleased*) A feast?

QUEEN:
The thought may jar

But it's written in the stars

Your daughter is marrying the Beast

KING:
The Beast!

REST OF CAST:
(*who have danced their way on stage*)
His daughter is marrying the Beast

QUEEN:
The Beast is actually a Prince

KING:
A Prince?

QUEEN:
What's happened will make you want to wince

KING:
To wince?

QUEEN:
He's the victim of a spell

But a kiss will make all well

For the Beast is actually a Prince

REST OF CAST:
The Beast is actually a Prince

QUEEN:
Rapunzel's the girl to set him free

KING:
Set him free?

QUEEN:
Your brother has made the prophecy

KING:
Prophecy?

QUEEN:
A kiss will do the trick
It will all be very quick
Rapunzel's the girl to set him free

REST OF CAST:
Rapunzel's the girl to set him free

QUEEN:
And then they'll realise they're in love

KING:
(*pleased*) They're in love!

QUEEN:
There'll be bluebirds singing up above

KING:
Up above? (*he looks up, anxiously*)

QUEEN:
The two of them will wed
And they'll hurry off to …..

CHORUS:
Waitrose to do their shopping

QUEEN:
Then they'll realise they're in love

REST OF CAST:
Then they'll realise they're in love

QUEEN:
The end is happiness and joy

KING:
(*pleased*) And joy!

QUEEN:
She'll give birth to a lovely little boy

KING:
A boy?

QUEEN:
A princely little beast
And when you're long deceased

KING:
Eh?

QUEEN:
The end will be happiness and joy

REST OF CAST:
The end will be happiness and joy

KING:
Hold on to a sec!

REST OF CAST:
The end will be happiness and joy
Happiness and joy
Happiness and joy

(The Chorus dance off as they sing)

KING: Hey! I didn't like that bit at the end – about being long deceased!

QUEEN: I'm sure you're good for a few more years yet Horace.

KING: I should jolly well hope so! Anyway – well sung my dear!

QUEEN: Thank you. And I hope you understand now the importance of what I've been saying. About Rapunzel marrying the Beast?

KIN: Ah. Yes. I think so dear. I wasn't actually listening much to the words. It's the music I like best. *(He hums a bit of the song)* "Your daughter's marrying the Beast…"

RAPUNZEL: (*entering*) Daddy – have you heard what Tiresias has been –

KING: (*startled*) Who the hell are you? You can't just come barging into the Royal Throne Room you know. I'll have your head cut off!

RAPUNZEL: Don't be silly Daddy! I'm your daughter, Rapunzel. Sister of Shirley.

KING: Nonsense! I know who Rapunzel is. She's got oodles of hair for starters. It goes down all the way to her……you know…. and way beyond it actually. You can't see her for hair – it's all over the place.

RAPUNZEL: I've had it cut off Daddy. Most of it.

QUEEN: And a good thing too!

KING: Why? Your hair was the best thing about you. It's not as if you've got much of a face.

RAPUNZEL: Daddy! That's a horrid thing to say -

KING: (*sitting on his throne again*) And anyway – what about the prophecy Thingy made? About some handsome fellow shinning up your hair and marrying you.

QUEEN: That prophecy is way past its sell-by date Horace!

RAPUNZEL: Besides which Daddy, have you ever tried letting down your hair for hunking great brutes to clamber up it?

KING: Er no, I haven't actually. A bit difficult in my case.

RAPUNZEL: It's extremely painful let me tell you! They pull at your roots, they tear great tufts of it out in their hands – and they when finally get to you, they're almost always a disappointment.

QUEEN: Life's like that darling.

RAPUNZEL: Not a handsome young Prince for love nor money! Overweight and tongue-tied most of them. And when they do open their mouths, all they want to do is talk about themselves.

QUEEN: That's men for you.

RAPUNZEL: Apart from Jack of course. He was nice. I really liked him.

KING: Jack! The boy who ran off with his mother's money and frittered it away on a beanstalk. He was quite unworthy of your hand, and I told him so in no uncertain terms!

QUEEN: I hate to agree with your father darling, but he was totally unsuitable!

KING: There we are! Straight from the horse's mouth!

QUEEN: I beg your -

RAPUNZEL: But he was kind! He was brave. And he was a good kisser! What more do you want in a man, Daddy?

KING: Money for starters.

RAPUNZEL: There's more things to life than money!

KING: You can't buy muffins with bravery and good kissing Rachel!

RAPUNZEL: Rapunzel!

KING: (*getting up sharply and looking round*) Where?

QUEEN: But darling – haven't you heard? Tiresias has now prophesied you're to marry the Beast!

RAPUNZEL: (*horrified*) The Beast who lives on the hill!? The weirdo who likes to drink the blood of children and fresh young partridges with his porridge.

QUEEN: I'm sure that's just an old wives' tale darling.

KING: Well you're an old wife! You should know! (*laughs*)

QUEEN: (*gritted teeth*) I'm a *young* wife Horace. A young *second* wife. Married to a very rude *old* man.

KING: Of course dear. You're absolutely right. Sorry.

RAPUNZEL: Well I'm not going anywhere near that beast, I can promise you that.

QUEEN: But he won't be a beast after you've kissed him darling. .

RAPUNZEL: (*even more horrified*) Me, kiss him! You've got to be joking!

QUEEN: He'll turn immediately into a handsome Prince! You'll have released him from his enchantment. And he'll fall in love with you at once.

KING: You'd be better-looking with more hair, mind.

QUEEN: Oh do be quiet Horace! Now Rapunzel - I promise you darling, one quick kiss will change your life for ever!

RAPUNZEL: Step-mummy I'm telling you; you and Daddy can talk until you're blue in the face, but nothing - absolutely *nothing* you say - is going to persuade me to visit the Beast and *kiss* him. And that's that.

KING: Well that's the end of the play then…. *(to the audience)* You lot might as well all trot off home. I'm going to ring for some more muffins. (*He goes to pull a hairy bell cord. We hear bell ring in distance*)

RAPUNZEL: *(noticing the cord)* Hey! That's my hair you're pulling!

KING: (*surprised*) Really?

QUEEN: Waste not, want not dear. It makes a very good bellpull.

RAPUNZEL: Honestly! Well I'm off to visit Granny. I've baked her some nice muffins for her birthday.

KING: Muffins?

QUEEN: That's nice -

RAPUNZEL: It's a long journey through the woods and I'm late already. 'Bye!

KING: (*jovially*) Don't get eaten by the big bad wolf! (*laughs*)

RAPUNZEL: Don't be ridiculous Daddy! This isn't a fairy tale. (S*he leaves*)

Pause

KING: Well – that went well, didn't it?

QUEEN: She just needs some gentle persuasion Horace.

KING: Mmmm…..

QUEEN: If you tell her that if she doesn't kiss the Beast you're going to throw her out of the castle, bag and baggage, without a penny to her name, I'm sure she can be persuaded to change her mind.

KING: I say – that's a little harsh my dear?

QUEEN: It's for her own good Horace! When she finds the Beast is really a handsome Prince, she'll be happy as Larry.

KING: Larry who?

QUEEN: Oh for Heaven's sake!

KING: *(pulls bell chord again. Bell rings again in distance)* Where on earth is the muffin fellow? I think *his* name's Larry. *(He turns to a member of the audience)* Have you seen the muffin man?

(Waits for response)

KING: No? Really? You know that reminds me of a song I used to sing when I was a child. *(He sings – with increasing enthusiasm)* Have you seen the muffin man, the muffin man, the muffin man? Have you seen the muffin man – he lives down

BEAST

Drury Lane. I've not seen the muffin man, the muffin man, I've not seen the…….

QUEEN: Oh stop making a fool of yourself Horace, in front of these good people.

KING: *(taking in audience for the first time)* Sorry! Sorry! *(sotto)* Who are they, by the way, and what are they doing here?

QUEEN: They're the audience!

KING: The audience! In the Royal Throne Room! That's outrageous!

QUEEN: This is a play Horace….plays need audiences. Not that this one looks up to much.

KING: Don't I know it's a play! This is my one and only scene – can you believe it? What sort of idiotic writer would create such a magnificent creature as me - the King - only to get rid of him after one miserable scene!!

QUEEN: Well what about me! The Queen! I've hardly got another speech either.

KING: *(to a member of the audience)* You little girl. You don't want me, the King, to disappear after one scene do you?

(Hopefully, she'll say ' no')

KING: No of course you don't. There we are then. That's democracy for you. I'll be back. That'll teach that stupid writer a thing or two about how to construct plays.

QUEEN: Indeed.

KING: Anyway – we must say a fond farewell to these good people. I've got furniture to move before the next scene.

QUEEN: Well don't trip over your feet like you did yesterday.

KING: It's almost impossible to see anything you know in the blackout. *(Blackout – but King continues talking)* No! no! Not yet. That wasn't your cue! Oh Gobstoppers! You just can't get the staff….*(We hear him trip over)* There! What did I tell you! *(He trips again)* Ow! OW!!! For Heaven's sake! Play some music somebody!

MUSIC

Halfway through music lights go up and RAPUNZEL and ROYAL SOOTHSAYER enter and wander through forest. Once music ends bring in sound of wild wood - continue this until Rapunzel's song

SCENE 2 – THE WILD WOOD

RAPUNZEL: Which way Daddy?

ROYAL SOOTHSAYER: *(He points at the cap he is wearing, speaking in a broad Scottish accent, through gritted teeth)* I'm not your Daddy! I'm not the King! I'm Tiresias the Royal Soothsayer!!

RAPUNZEL: Of course you are! Sorry. It's just that you look so like Daddy.

ROYAL SOOTHSAYER: That's because I'm his *twin brother*…(*unconvincingly*) Born five minutes after him, and to stop any confusion sent to live for thirty seven years with our Aunty Jean in Glasgow, which explains my Scottish accent. *(coming out of character)* Honestly, how am I expected to say a line like that and make it *real*? Make it *truthful*. I've worked for the Royal Shakespeare Company you know…

RAPUNZEL: *(out of character)* No you haven't Neil. *(or whoever is playing the character)*

ROYAL SOOTHSAYER: Well I *could* have done!!

RAPUNZEL: Anyway - enough of that…..Can you believe it Tiresias, I'm going to be thrown out of the castle, bag and baggage, without a penny-

ROYAL SOOTHSAYER: Hippopotamus!

RAPUNZEL: - to my name, if I don't go and kiss the Beast. And it's all absolutely pointless!

ROYAL SOOTHSAYER: Hippopotamus!

RAPUNZEL: Must you say Hippopotamus every time I speak?

ROYAL SOOTHSAYER: I do apologise your Royal Highness. It's just this curse the Witch has put – Hippopotamus - on me again. Every time anybody says a word beginning with P – Hippopotamus - I'm forced to say -

RAPUNZEL: Hippopotamus!

ROYAL SOOTHSAYER: Precisely. Hippopotamus!

RAPUNZEL: Oh dear. Well I shall try and avoid words beginning with…that letter….in the future

ROYAL SOOTHSAYER: That's most kind of you Princess Hippopotamus!

RAPUNZEL: And I'd be grateful if you could try and do the same.

ROYAL SOOTHSAYER: Absolutely, Princess Hippopotamus! Oops! Sorry…sorry….

RAPUNZEL: Look if you must call me anything, call me Rapunzel.

ROYAL SOOTHSAYER: I shall stick to Your Royal Highness, Your Royal Highness. It's much more polite. Hippopotamus! Sorry, sorry. Look, we'd better get on. It's this way….I think… *(They walk on)*

RAPUNZEL: What did you do to upset the Witch this time?

ROYAL SOOTHSAYER: She accused me of leaving her broomstick out in the rain, when she'd asked me to bring it in.

RAPUNZEL: And had you?

ROYAL SOOTHSAYER: Well….possibly….Hippopotamus! But so what? She has a few wet twigs to contend with! She's a *witch* isn't she? She can magic up another broomstick – rather than take out her bad temper on me.

RAPUNZEL: Auntie Bertha's a little out of sorts Tiresias. She just needs the love of a good man. Or even a bad one.

ROYAL SOOTHSAYER: I'm sorry my Lady – I know she's your aunt – but I'd like the Beast to gobble her up. They say he eats witches for breakfast….

RAPUNZEL: Not to mention the odd Soothsayer….

ROYAL SOOTHSAYER: No – let's not mention the odd Soothsayer *(He shudders – he's frightened of the Beast)* I tell you honestly Your Royal Highness, I'm not looking forward at all to this encounter…

RAPUNZEL: It's your own fault Tiresias. If you hadn't made this prophecy

ROYAL SOOTHSAYER: Hippopotamus!

RAPUNZEL: Er……prediction

ROYAL SOOTHSAYER: Hippopotamus!

RAPUNZEL: If you hadn't said I was going to marry the Beast, Step Mummy and Daddy wouldn't have forced me to travel to the castle with you to meet him.

ROYAL SOOTHSAYER: Well I can't help it Your Royal Highness. These sooths that I say, I don't just make them up you know.

RAPUNZEL: No of course you don't.

ROYAL SOOTHSAYER: There's years of training goes into it, if one's going to be soothful. A great deal of mucking around with eye of newt, toe of frog....that sort of thing.

RAPUNZEL: Ugh!

ROYAL SOOTHSAYER: Shall we sit down for a moment Your Royal Highness. Have a little rest?

RAPUNZEL: What a good idea!

ROYAL SOOTHSAYER: *(plonking himself down on the only available tree stump, much to the Princess's disgust)* You see in my job, you have to distinguish between sooths and half-sooths.

RAPUNZEL: Well with all due respect Tiresias, you don't have much of a track-record, do you?

ROYAL SOOTHSAYER: What do you mean by that?

RAPUNZEL: Nine months, thanks to you, I was imprisoned in our castle turret, letting my hair down to this fellow and that, and there was only one young man whom I could remotely imagine marrying.

ROYAL SOOTHSAYER: I admit that particular sooth was a little unsoothful -

RAPUNZEL: It wasn't soothful at all! Nor was that sleeping sooth.

ROYAL SOOTHSAYER: Er...remind me of that one your Royal Highness.

RAPUNZEL: Three months of my life wasted, fast asleep, while waiting for some handsome young man to wake me up with a kiss.

ROYAL SOOTHSAYER: Ah, yes...that sleeping sooth.

RAPUNZEL: And as for that ridiculous business with the pea!

ROYAL SOOTHSAYER: Hippopotamus!

RAPUNZEL: Sorry – tiny green vegetable....I used to get vertigo from having to climb up thirteen mattresses to get into my bed each night.

ROYAL SOOTHSAYER: Very distressing for you.

RAPUNZEL: You could have stuck a cabbage, a cauliflower, and the hind leg of a donkey under twelve mattresses, and I wouldn't have felt them!

ROYAL SOOTHSAYER: I do apologise Your Royal Highness!

There's a menacing roar from the distance

RAPUNZEL: Oh my – what on earth was that?

ROYAL SOOTHSAYER: *(getting up hurriedly from his stump)* It's the Beast Your Royal Highness.

RAPUNZEL: The Beast?

ROYAL SOOTHSAYER: They say he generally has a mid-afternoon roar or two from his castle battlement. It helps his digestion.

RAPUNZEL: And that's the man I have to kiss? Oh I feel so depressed. *(She moves the stump towards her and sits down)*

The BEAST roars again

ROYAL SOOTHSAYER: I don't feel too happy either. *(He goes to sit on his stump again, not realising it's no longer there, and falls over..)* Ow!!

RAPUNZEL: You know what? I'm going to sing a song to help cheer myself up. *(He gets up. Shouts to nobody in particular)* Where's my music *(music intro starts)* I always find singing a great help in times of distress.

ROYAL SOOTHSAYER: *(still suffering)* Pilchards! Ow! Hippopotamus!

Song – *"I'm Afraid of the Beast"*

RAPUNZEL:
I'd rather be me than be you
I know people think
A Princess
Has success
More or less
And that's true.

ROYAL SOOTHSAYER:
Hippopotamus

RAPUNZEL:
But you know
For I've only just now told you so
That my life isn't quite what I want
For a dare
Men climbed up my hair
And now it's not there
It's a blow
I just want a good man
That's my major life-plan

ROYAL SOOTHSAYER:
Hippopotamus

RAPUNZEL:
It may seem a bit shallow to you
But for me
Hear my plea

ROYAL SOOTHSAYER:
Hippopotamus

RAPUNZEL:
Set me free
Tell me you can
And I'll even kiss the vile Beast
If it hastens my own wedding feast
I shall do just whatever it takes
He can bite
He can fight
It's all right
I wouldn't mind in the least

The other two cast members appear out of nowhere to provide a chorus

CHORUS:
She wouldn't mind in the least ...Except....

PRINCESS:
Except… I'm afraid of the Beast
CHORUS:
She's afraid of the Beast *(They dance off)*

ROYAL SOOTHSAYER: Oh don't be afraid of him my Lady.

RAPUNZEL: Why not?

ROYAL SOOTHSAYER: I'm sure all these tales of him roaming the forest at night and slaughtering and eating anything that moves are just folk having a bit of a laugh..

RAPUNZEL: *(not reassured at all)* Well, that's reassuring to know ….

A fierce roar from the Beast is heard in the distance

RAPUNZEL: Ahhh!

ROYAL SOOTHSAYER: *(trance-like for a moment)* Beware! Beware!

His flashing eyes, his floating hair!

Weave a circle round him thrice

And close your eyes with holy dread

For he on honeydew hath fed,

And drunk the milk of Paradise.

Hippopotamus.

RAPUNZEL: Wow! That's brilliant Tiresias! Who said that?

ROYAL SOOTHSAYER: I did. Right – well we'd better get a move on if we're to reach the castle before dark. I'll go and scout ahead.

RAPUNZEL: Don't leave me alone! You know what my father said…..Tiresias! Tiresias! *(but he has already disappeared)*

And who should appear but her father – Tiresias having hurriedly changed his hat

KING: Ah - there you are Sheila….Shelley…..Shirley

RAPUNZEL: *(irritated)* Rapunzel!

KING: Rapunzel. That's what I said wasn't it. *(to audience)* Wasn't it? No?

RAPUNZEL: What are you doing here anyway Daddy? You're not in this scene.

KING: Hah! That's where you're wrong my girl! That stupid writer's not limiting me to one miserly scene. I'll show him.

RAPUNZEL: But there'll be a blackout any moment

KING: Blackout?

There's a blackout

KING: *(to unseen stagehand)* No! No! I didn't mean *blackout!* - That wasn't an instruction you dunderhead!

RAPUNZEL: Never mind Daddy. You can help shift the scenery.

KING: Look I'm the King! I've got better things to do than *Ow! Ow!* For heaven's sake! I've tripped over something! Play some music somebody!

And again somebody does

SCENE 3 – THE BEAST'S PARLOUR

Light comes up on JACK, sweeping the floor. He looks up and notices the audience

JACK: Oh – hello! Don't mind me - I'm Jack, the Beast's manservant – I'm just sweeping up his lunch. Three French hens, two turtle doves and a partridge from his own pear tree…….. with pears for afters. *(turns to child in audience)* Would you like to help me sweep up this mess? No? I'm not surprised. There's nothing messier than a half-eaten French hen….Feathers all over the place…

I'm using the witch's broomstick – don't for heaven's sake tell her will you? She gets very cross if she finds people borrowing her things. She's a guest in the castle. Between you and me I think she's rather fond of the Beast, you know. Well – it takes all sorts.

Now – I know that it's not me you've come to see, is it? You've come to see the Beast haven't you? Well – you'll see him soon enough, but you're going to have to see the Witch first. And – a word of warning - our witch has a habit of turning people into tuna fish sandwiches. So it's best not to get on the wrong side of her. Mind you – she likes feisty folk – that's people who will stand up to her. So don't whatever you do act scared. My advice is to boo her loudly when she first comes on stage. That'll tell her you're not like the namby-pamby audience that we had yesterday. Most of them ended up between two slices of bread…

Shall we have a practice? I'll pretend to be the witch, making her first entrance, and you boo me, right? OK – imagine me dressed all in black with a pointy black hat – here I come…….

(Boos)

No no – that's not nearly good enough! Your boos have to be louder than that, otherwise you'll lose all her respect. Let's try again… OK….I'm coming….. I'm coming….

(Louder boos)

That's much better! Much better! Good! You'll be nicely prepared when she -

There's a loud knock on the castle door

Good heavens! Who could that be at this time of night? It can't be the Witch – she's having supper with the Beast. Any ideas anyone? *(responds appropriately to audience suggestion)* The Princess? Gosh, I hope you're right – I do hope so! Well we'll just have to see, won't we?

Opens castle door, leaving witch's broomstick on side

RAPUNZEL: *(very surprised)* Oh – hello.

JACK: *(gazing at her, love-struck)* Hello.

RAPUNZEL: You're –

JACK.: Yes. *(beat)* Yes I am.

RAPUNZEL: That's amazing.

JACK: Well I work here…

RAPUNZEL: Not so amazing then!

Pause while they drink each other in….

ROYAL SOOTHSAYER: *(impatiently)* I say. Any chance we could come in?

JACK: Oh, Of course. Of course. Sorry. Do step this way…

TIRESIAS: After you, Princess Hippopotamus.

RAPUNZEL: Thank you.

Beat

JACK: What are you doing now?

RAPUNZEL: I'm still a Princess

ROYAL SOOTHSAYER: Hippopotamus!!

JACK: Please –

ROYAL SOOTHSAYER: Hippopotamus!

JACK: Er – Princess?

ROYAL SOOTHSAYER: Hippopotamus!

RAPUNZEL: Oh don't mind Tiresias. My Auntie Bertha, who's a witch, has put a curse on him, so that every time someone says a word beginning with the letter in the alphabet after 'O' -

JACK: *(helpfully)* P?

ROYAL SOOTHSAYER: Hippopotamus!!

RAPUNZEL: He says… *(very quietly)* Hippopotamus

JACK: Pardon?

ROYAL SOOTHSAYER & RAPUNZEL: *(together)* Hippopotamus!

JACK: Ah! Right.

RAPUNZEL: Look Tiresias – could you leave us alone for a little while? We've got a few things we need to catch up on.

ROYAL SOOTHSAYER: I'm sorry your Royal Highness, King Horace expressly told me not to leave your side for a single minute……not a *single* minute!

There's a loud noise from off stage

RAPUNZEL: Ah! Is that the Beast I hear coming downstairs?

JACK: Probably.

ROYAL SOOTHSAYER: *(nervously)* Hippopotamus…… On the other hand, I may need to go to the loo for a moment…. So if you'll excuse me both of you…I'll be back as quickly as ……I can. Which way should I? *(another roar)* Never mind…. *(He exits, quickly)*

Beat

JACK: He's frightened of the Beast your man, isn't he? I can tell.

RAPUNZEL: Yes. Yes he is a bit. So am I actually.

JACK: No need. The Beast's as gentle as a young lamb really. Except to young lambs!

RAPUNZEL: *(sheepish laugh)*

JACK: Please – do sit down Princess.

RAPUNZEL: Thank you. Thank you. *(She sits on the one available chair)*

JACK: Sorry – we only have the one chair. The Beast doesn't have many visitors– and we didn't have the budget for two….

Beat

JACK: So….Princess. You've had your hair cut.

RAPUNZEL: I cut it off myself actually.

JACK: When was that?

RAPUNZEL: A couple of weeks ago. I'd hung it out of the top window of the castle turret as Tiresias instructed, and I looked down and saw this long-haired loon, with a red face and a pot belly start to claw his way up my hair, and I thought …

JACK: Enough's enough!

RAPUNZEL: Enough's enough! So I took a big pair of scissors and….Bob's your uncle!

JACK: He is actually! Good old Uncle Bob! What happened to the long-haired loon?

RAPUNZEL: Well – let's say he came down to earth with a bump! *(they laugh)* Honestly - I've had my fill of young men using my hair as a rope ladder.

JACK: I'm sorry -

RAPUNZEL: No no….I didn't mind *you* . Honestly. You were different from all the others. You were so gentle and kind. You didn't hurt me a bit.

JACK: Well – I'd had a bit of training hadn't I? Shinning up your lovely hair was a doddle compared to clambering up that beanstalk. I just wish….

RAPUNZEL: What?

JACK: Well…..that your father might have treated me a little more kindly

RAPUNZEL: He liked you. I'm sure he did. He just said he thought I should be marrying someone a little –

JACK: Richer. Yes, I know. He told me next time I climbed a beanstalk I should come back with a shedload of money….

RAPUNZEL: You were so brave doing it. Is it true you met a giant?

JACK: Yeah. And his wife. A nice couple. They invited me in for tea. The wife served me a rock cake twice as big as my head!

RAPUNZEL: I was told they tried to eat you alive.

JACK: Nah! They couldn't have been nicer. People talk an awful lot of rot about giants.

RAPUNZEL: But what about the golden egg you stole?

JACK: I didn't steal any golden egg. The giant's wife gave me an egg to take back to my Mum, and it was so heavy I dropped it on my way down the beanstalk.

RAPUNZEL: Oh.

JACK: That's probably how the rumours started. Someone found an eggshell, someone else said it was made of gold, and before you could say Jack Robinson, I'm supposed to have stolen a golden egg, and made my fortune.

RAPUNZEL: Is that your name – Jack Robinson?

JACK: Yes – but please just call me Jack.

RAPUNZEL: So - you're working here now….Jack.

JACK: Yeah. The Beast pays well and it's a good steady job.

RAPUNZEL: But isn't he very frightening?

JACK: Well – it's best to keep on the right side of him. But he's nothing like as frightening as people say he is.

(The BEAST roars)

RAPUNZEL: He sounds pretty frightening to me….

Beat

JACK: So why have you come here Princess? I bet it wasn't to see me.

RAPUNZEL: Well – don't laugh. I've come to kiss the Beast!

JACK: You've come to do what?

RAPUNZEL: I'm not looking forward to it very much

JACK: So why do it?

RAPUNZEL: It's been prophesied. The Beast is actually a handsome Prince, and if I kiss him I can release him from his enchantment.

JACK: Wow! I always thought there was something rather noble about him you know. That would explain it.

RAPUNZEL: He's never said anything to you? About once being a Prince?

JACK: Not a word.

RAPUNZEL: I expect the enchantment made him completely forget about his former life

JACK: That would explain it. Yes. Still –

RAPUNZEL: What?

JACK: I don't like….

RAPUNZEL: What don't you like?

JACK: The thought of you kissing him….

RAPUNZEL: It could be dangerous you mean?

JACK: No, no. It's just….

RAPUNZEL: Just what?

Song: A Mess of One's life

JACK:
A mess -

A mess of my life

Oh Princess, I confess, it's a mess that I've made of my life….

For there's nothing, no nothing, I want more than you as my wife.

But your father is right, that the sight of a man such as me,

Would offend, be the end - of that I can quite guarantee.

RAPUNZEL:
My dear Jack, don't look back, you're a man one should envy and praise.

I despair, but it's rare to find someone like you nowadays.

To my mind, you are kind - and considerate too.

What more to look for should one want, but a person like you?

BOTH:
It's a shame, none's to blame, but we're simply the people we are.

We are trapped, can't adapt, handicapped by own guiding star.

JACK:
I was born in a slum - and my Mum had a miserable life,

RAPUNZEL:
I was born a Princess but must make a success as a wife.

RAPUNZEL:
I am rich

JACK:
I am poor

BOTH:
But it's you I adore.

RAPUNZEL:
Tell me once more -

JACK:
Yes it's you I adore.

RAPUNZEL:
You said that before

Beat

BOTH
(*sadly*) Don't let's sing…. Anymore…..
Sing - no more.

JACK: Oh Rapunzel-

RAPUNZEL: You don't like the idea of me kissing him, do you?

JACK: It's not that….

RAPUNZEL: What then?

JACK: I just hoped –

RAPUNZEL: What?

JACK: That if there was any kissing to be done…..you might have wanted to kiss….somebody else.

RAPUNZEL: Do you think….somebody else….would have minded me kissing him?

JACK: Not at all. I think he would have been….absolutely thrilled.

(They're very close to each other by now, but back away guiltily as the ROYAL SOOTHSAYER barges in)

ROYAL SOOTHSAYER: Sorry! Sorry! Couldn't find my way back from the loo! It's big this castle, isn't it?

JACK: No bigger than most castles.

ROYAL SOOTHSAYER: Yes – but most castles are big, aren't they? That's the thing about castles. Their bigness.

JACK: I suppose so.

ROYAL SOOTHSAYER: I can't remember the last time I was in a small castle!

JACK: No.

ROYAL SOOTHSAYER: I mean there must *be* small castles. It's just that I haven't been in any.

RAPUNZEL: Right.

ROYAL SOOTHSAYER: Not yet, anyway.

JACK: No.

(Pause)

ROYAL SOOTHSAYER: Has he been down yet?

RAPUNZEL: Who?

ROYAL SOOTHSAYER: The Beast of course.

JACK: The Beast is having an after-dinner cigar with the Witch.

ROYAL SOOTHSAYER: *(relieved)* Ah well in that case we'd better be off, hadn't we? We don't want to disturb him when he's –

JACK: Not at all! Let me get you something to eat and drink, and then I'll take you up to see him.

ROYAL SOOTHSAYER: That's most kind of you.

RAPUNZEL: Will you stay with us when we're with him Jack?

JACK: Oh no – I can't do that.

RAPUNZEL: Why not?

ROYAL SOOTHSAYER: Yes – why not?

JACK: Well - two reasons really. For one thing the Beast is a very shy man. Too many folks at any one time might upset him you know.

RAPUNZEL: Oh...

JACK: And you wouldn't want to see him upset....

ROYAL SOOTHSAYER: *(fearful)* No, no we certainly wouldn't…..

RAPUNZEL: And the other thing? You said there were two reasons…

JACK: Well - I'm also the actor playing the Beast you see - so it simply wouldn't be possible!

RAPUNZEL& ROYAL SOOTHSAYER: *(look at each other)* Hippopotamus!

BLACKOUT & MUSIC

SCENE 4 – THE WILD WOOD

WITCH: *(enters looking cross)* Hello….hello…. Anybody seen my broomstick? (S*he's greeted, as* Jack *suggested, by a volley of boos*)

Watch it you lot! You won't intimidate me with your booing. I'm a fully-fledged card-carrying witch you know! Not some old biddy, down on her luck, whom you might see in the rain outside Tesco's. (*singles out child*) Have you ever met a witch dear? No? Well look round this audience – I can see several likely witches here…. Those Ladies from Wimbledon Common Golf Club (*choose your victims*) for instance – every one of them a witch from what I've heard. Now anyone here called (*She names a child that has been picked out beforehand*) Ever thought of becoming one? No? Have you got a broom at home? Well buy yourself one and you're halfway there. You could be an apprentice witch and work for me, dear. Can you cook? My cat Matilda does the cooking at home. She's awful. She serves me the same dish every day. Fried Mice followed by Mice Cream. I tell you there's a limit to how many times you can eat Fried Mice in a week. It's the tails I can't stand. They wiggle about even after they've been cooked you know….. Puts you right off your meal.

Now listen. I've got my own song. Do you want to hear it? Well I don't care whether you do or not. It's my song, and I'm going to sing it! Music now!

Witch's Song

WITCH:
You don't get rich,
Being a witch….
But it's fun.
You don't get rich
Being a Witch.
For if I give my wand a twirl
I can turn you little girl
Into a scrumptious currant bun.
O yes I could – perhaps I should
Get on my broom ,

Fly round this room
And make a chicken casserole of
Everyone....

But don't despair.
I'm very fair
Ask anyone.
But don't despair.
I'm very fair.
If you treat me with respect,
Admire my fearsome intellect,
Then we'll have fun.
In retrospect
We'll have a ball.
But if you make me hopping mad
I can be very, very bad
Turn your fingers into butter,
Throw your toys into the gutter,
Every one...

Every Witch
Must have a cat
I can't stand mine.
For every witch must have a cat
My cat is called Matilda
Several times I've nearly killed her
But then again, a cat has got nine lives.
She is lazy and pernicious
And occasionally vicious
A crazy mixed-up mog
Who thinks she is a dog
Can you believe it?

But I'm so glad
That I'm so bad

> It's a laugh.
> Yes, I'm so glad
> That I'm bad.
> I gave myself three wishes
> Never wash or dry the dishes
> I never floss between my teeth
> Nor have a bath.
> My bedroom's a disgrace
> Looks like someone's trashed the place,
> But nothing goes to waste
> Cos my magic spells are ace!
> Yes, I'm a witch! A lovely witch!
> Yes, I'm a witch! I'm a witch, I'm a wi…..tch. I'm a WITCH!

WITCH: There. Great wasn't it! Adele – eat your heart out! Or maybe the Beast would do it for me. He's a real man the Beast! Not the sort of lily-livered young fellow that your elder sister might go out with! Those boys wouldn't say boo to a goose. My Beast would tear the goose limb from limb and eat him with his breakfast Shreddies!

Now then – what was my broom doing over there? Who put it there? Answer me? Answer me?

Jack?! Don't try and put the blame on Jack! He wouldn't dare take my broom. It was one of you, wasn't it? Go on – admit it! Stand up the person who took my broom! *(pause)* OK. I've given you a chance. I'm now going to turn you all into tuna fish sandwiches! There! *(FX: magic sting)* That's taught you all a lesson, hasn't it! *(beat)*

What do you mean it hasn't worked! Of course it's worked. A tuna fish sandwich spell is one of the most difficult spells a witch can do – it takes several hours before anything happens. You'll all be tuna fish sandwiches at precisely *(looks at her watch)* four-fifteen this afternoon. My advice – keep away from the cat! *(she cackles happily)*

Right then – I'm off to see the Beast. I've heard a very unpleasant rumour that young Rapunzel has been sent to try and remove the Beast's enchantment with a kiss, and I plan to put a stop to that!

KING: (*arriving hurriedly from auditorium out of breath*) Bertha! Bertha!

WITCH: (*surprised*) Horace! What are you doing here? This is my scene and it's for me only. You've no business interrupting my monologue…

KING: But I've come all the way from the Palace -

WITCH: Well that's too bad , but you've got no lines in this scene, and I'm just making my exit. After which there's a Blackout! *(blackout)* There!

KING: Oh – not again!

WITCH: You can help change the scenery.

KING: I've said before – Kings don't change the scenery! I can't see a pesky thing. Ow! I've tripped over again! Bertha! Bertha! Get them to play some more music!

And more music is played until lights come up on next scene.

SCENE 5 – THE BEAST'S DRAWING ROOM

The ROYAL SOOTHSAYER and RAPUNZEL are sitting together nervously on a settee

ROYAL SOOTHSAYER: How much longer must we wait your Royal Highness? The Beast must have finished his supper by now.

RAPUNZEL: Come, come Tiresias. Have a little patience.

ROYAL SOOTHSAYER: *(quietly)* Hippopotamus. We should never have come you know. Whose stupid idea was it to visit the Beast in his own castle?

RAPUNZEL: It was yours.

ROYAL SOOTHSAYER: Possibly. Hippopotamus.

RAPUNZEL: The prophecy.

ROYAL SOOTHSAYER: Hippopotamus.

RAPUNZEL: Oh I do wish you'd stop saying -

ROYAL SOOTHSAYER: *(getting up - exploding)* So do I! So do I! Oh Your Royal Highness! You've no idea the anguish it causes me. *(calls out)* Music maestro! *(hippo music played)*

Let me explain …

Song: The Hippopotamus Song

ROYAL SOOTHSAYER:
I feel such a silly clotamus, an awful idiotamus
Always finishing sentences by saying hippopotamus
It's such a silly word, and it's really quite absurd
I try hard not to say it, but I fear that I cannotamus….
Hippopotamus!

ALL JOIN IN FOR FOLLOWING VERSES:
Everywhere you go you hear an awful lot of rotamus
About the noble qualities this animal has gotamus.
He rolls around in mud, he's a thorough-going dud

An amazing smelly waste of space, a complete and absolute disgrace
Hippopotamus!

My favourite flower has always been the wild forgetmenotamus
My favourite living creature is the fearsome ocelotamus
But I couldn't give a fig, however small or big
For that ugly looking animal - I'd really like to ban 'em all
The Hippopotamus!

My favourite fruit, I'd like one now's, a juicy apricotamus
My favourite bird, lives by the sea's a lovely guillemotamus
But the creature I despise, it will come as no surprise
Is that good for nothing thimblerig, that dirty-looking jumped-up pig...
AAHHGH! Hippopotamus!

He feels such a silly clotamus, an awful idiotamus
Always finishing sentences by saying hippopotamus
It's the creature we despise, it will come as no surprise
Is that good for nothing thimblerig, that dirty-looking jumped-up pig
...AAHHGH! Hippopotamus!
Oh Yeah!

(They dance off)

ROYAL SOOTHSAYER: *(going back to sit with PRINCESS)* I try hard not to say it...

RAPUNZEL: But you fear that you cannotnotamus. Yes - I sympathise. I really do Tiresias. When I next see Auntie Bertha I'll try and get her to reverse the spell.

ROYAL SOOTHSAYER: Oh thank you Your Royal Highness!

RAPUNZEL: It'll be a pleasure.

ROYAL SOOTHSAYER: Hippopotamus!

There's a frightening-blood-curdling roar from offstage.

ROYAL SOOTHSAYER: Good Heavens – what was that?

RAPUNZEL: It must be the Beast.

ROYAL SOOTHSAYER: *(scared witless)* That roar! It sends shivers up my you know what....

RAPUNZEL: And mine!

ROYAL SOOTHSAYER: My lady – you will look after me, won't you?

RAPUNZEL: You're meant to be looking after me!

Then another horrendous roar, slightly nearer.

RAPUNZEL: What are you doing Tiresias? Tiresias!

ROYAL SOOTHSAYER: *(He has rushed off stage to sit with the audience)* What does it look like? I'm trying to hide, aren't I.

RAPUNZEL: You can't sit in the audience

ROYAL SOOTHSAYER: Why not? *(turns to child)* You don't mind, do you? You could look after me, couldn't you? Shove up a bit. What's your name?

Audience member ……….

ROYAL SOOTHSAYER: ………….eh? You can always trust somebody called …………

RAPUNZEL: You can't sit there! You haven't bought a ticket! And why try anyway? The Beast knows we're here -

ROYAL SOOTHSAYER: You could say I had to leave rather suddenly. I had a message my wife was ill.

RAPUNZEL: You haven't got a wife.

ROYAL SOOTHSAYER: He's not to know that.

One final roar very close - ROYAL SOOTHSAYER & RAPUNZEL scream and ROYAL SOOTHSAYER runs from the audience and jumps into RAPUNZEL'S arms, terrified. THE BEAST enters with a megaphone in his right hand

BEAST: *(cheerfully)* Ah – Hello there!

ROYAL SOOTHSAYER: *(desperately trying to extricate himself from RAPUNZEL)* Oh hello…we were just…..

BEAST: Yes – I can see that. Now you must be Rapunzel and you must be the Royal Soothsayer. Jack told me you were waiting for me.

ROYAL SOOTHSAYER: *(trembling)* Er… That's right your Beastness.

BEAST: Sorry about the roaring! Hope I didn't scare you.

ROYAL SOOTHSAYER: *(mock bravery)* No, no – not at all!

BEAST: The neighbours expect it you know. I can't let them down.

RAPUNZEL: What do you mean?

BEAST: Well – as the only Beast in the immediate vicinity, I have to act up a bit you know. Loud roars from time to time. A bit of wild cavorting on castle battlements. All that allied to the rumours I've spread about eating young children doused in the blood of freshly killed partridges.

ROYAL SOOTHSAYER: Hippopotamus.

BEAST: Bless you.

RAPUNZEL: You mean you don't eat children doused in the blood of freshly killed partridges?

ROYAL SOOTHSAYER: Hippopotamus

BEAST: Good Lord no! I can't imagine anything more revolting. I like a cheese omelette followed by apple-crumble and ice cream.

RAPUNZEL: So why all the acting?

BEAST: Well. It's easiest if I sing you my reply to that. I take it you've no objection.

RAPUNZEL: Not at all – we both enjoy a good song.

BEAST: Right. Let's have some music then! *(music)* And – both of you – feel free to join in the chorus. Right here we go then:

Song: I Enjoy Being a Beast

BEAST:
I'm not the sort that anyone can just ignore
I scare the neighbours when I make a beastly roar
And when I fall asleep I've got the most appalling snore *(he snores)*
Inside the truth is clear to see...
I enjoy being a Beast

CHORUS:
(who have danced on) He enjoys being a Beast

BEAST:
I enjoy being a Beast

CHORUS:
He enjoys being a Beast
BEAST:
People say "you're as ugly as a pig!"
ROYAL SOOTHSAYER:
Hippopotamus!
BEAST:
But I don't mind- I couldn't give a fig
Pour me some champagne, I think I'd like another swig
Inside the truth is clear to see...
I enjoy being a Beast
CHORUS:
He enjoys being a Beast
BEAST:
I enjoy being a Beast
CHORUS:
He enjoys being a Beast
BEAST:
When I go shopping everybody starts to run
The streets are all deserted, you won't see anyone
I'm never charged for anything, 'cos I'm busy having fun
Inside the truth is clear to see...
I enjoy being a Beast
CHORUS:
He enjoys being a Beast
BEAST:
I enjoy being a Beast
CHORUS:
He enjoys being a Beast
BEAST:
I'm no beauty but I'm really not upset
White teeth to die for, and a face you won't forget
I'm really quite good-looking when you see my silhouette
Inside the truth is clear to see
I enjoy being a Beast

CHORUS:
He enjoys being a Beast

BEAST:
I enjoy being a Beast

CHORUS:
He enjoys being a Beast

BEAST:
(To audience) All together now!

BEAST:
I enjoy being a Beast

CHORUS:
He enjoys being a Beast

BEAST:
I enjoy being a Beast

CHORUS:
He enjoys being a Beast

BEAST:
Yeah!

ROYAL SOOTHSAYER: So you enjoy being a Beast then?

BEAST: Yes – you could say that. In fact you did say that didn't you. How did you know?

ROYAL SOOTHSAYER: *(fake modesty)* Well – I'm the Royal Soothsayer. It's my job to know things.

BEAST: Thanks for joining in by the way! It's much more fun than when I sing it by myself.

ROYAL SOOTHSAYER: *(He's relaxed a bit by now)* I love your gown.

BEAST: Yes – beastly, isn't it? Cost me an arm and leg that did. I forget whose arm and leg it was, but they were quite tasty.

ROYAL SOOTHSAYER: *(slightly worried again)* I thought you said you'd rather eat cheese omelettes?

BEAST: Well you have to vary your diet from time to time, don't you. Now, Jack's told me that you've come to kiss me, is that right?

ROYAL SOOTHSAYER: *(horrified)* Not me! I'm not kissing you!

BEAST: No – I didn't think it would be you.

ROYAL SOOTHSAYER: Mind you, I've kissed a few beasts in my time! Don't think I haven't.

RAPUNZEL: I've come to kiss you Mr Beast.

BEAST: And why might that be my dear?

ROYAL SOOTHSAYER: To remove your enchantment of course

RAPUNZEL: To turn you back into a handsome prince.

ROYAL SOOTHSAYER: Hippopotamus

BEAST: I don't actually remember ever having been a handsome prince –

ROYAL SOOTHSAYER: Hippopotamus

BEAST: Or even an ugly one for the matter. *(He sits on the Beast's chair)* Tell me, why all these hippopotami?

WITCH: *(entering unexpectedly)* It's because he's under one of my special curses, aren't you Tiresias?

BEAST: Oh - Hello Bertha

RAPUNZEL: Auntie!

ROYAL SOOTHSAYER: Oh no! It's you!

WITCH: It most certainly is! Peter Piper picked a peck of pickled peppers

ROYAL SOOTHSAYER: Hippopotamus, Hippopotamus, Hippopotamus, Hippopotamus, Hippopotamus, Hippopotamus.

RAPUNZEL: Oh Auntie do please remove the curse! It's driving me mad.

BEAST: Yes - give the old boy a break Bertha. He looks a decent enough cove.

BEAT

WITCH: Very well. I shall remove the curse, but only because you Beast have asked me to do it and I'm a guest in your Castle. *(bang)* There!

ROYAL SOOTHSAYER: Where's the peck of pickled peppers Peter Piper - Oh – that's brilliant. *(smiles as he realises he doesn't have to say hippopotamus)*

BEAST: Who's this Peter Piper chap?

WITCH: Just remember to treat people's personal property with a little more consideration next time Tiresias. *(beat)* But to more serious matters. This young woman has come, I believe, to remove your enchantment.

BEAST: Apparently.

ROYAL SOOTHSAYER: She's fulfilling a top-notch prophecy of mine you understand. Not for the first time.

WITCH: Do you want to be kissed by her, Gerald?

ROYAL SOOTHSAYER AND RAPUNZEL: Gerald?!

BEAST: *(getting off chair)* What's wrong with Gerald?

ROYAL SOOTHSAYER: You can't be a Beast and be called Gerald!

BEAST: I can and I am.

ROYAL SOOTHSAYER: I was once very close to a Gerald.

BEAST: Well you're close to him now – so just watch it!

WITCH: Boys! Boys! Behave.

ROYAL SOOTHSAYER: Gerald! *(all his fear of the Beast has now gone)*

WITCH: Now then. Answer the question Gerald. Do you want this young woman to kiss you?

BEAST: Well. I'm hardly going to refuse to be kissed by a gorgeous young woman am I?

WITCH: *(to RAPUNZEL)* And you Rapunzel? Do you want to kiss him?

RAPUNZEL: I feel it's my duty Auntie. To rid him of his enchantment.

ROYAL SOOTHSAYER: To turn him back into a handsome young Prince. Oh it's such a relief Princess not to have to say Hippopotamus!

WITCH: Be quiet, or I'll put the curse back.

ROYAL SOOTHSAYER: Sorry!

WITCH: Right. So you're going to rid him of his enchantment are you? Off you go then. Kiss him if you must.

RAPUNZEL: Really?

WITCH: Nothing too extravagant. There are children in the audience. *(she gestures to audience)*

RAPUNZEL: Right then. Well. Er Mr Beast….

BEAST: Call me Gerald

ROYAL SOOTHSAYER: *(mocking)* Gerald!

RAPUNZEL: Very well. Gerald…..Here goes. *(she plucks up courage and kisses him on the cheek)*

Pause

ROYAL SOOTHSAYER: Nothing's happened!

WITCH: So much for your prophecy.

ROYAL SOOTHSAYER: Sometimes these enchantment spells take a while to unravel….

WITCH: Rubbish! Now listen to me, all of you. You want to see a real spell? I'll give you one. *(to the BEAST)* Gerald, if you turn into a handsome Prince, are you ready to take this woman and make her your bride?

BEAST: Well – we hardly know each other, but she seems a very pleasant young woman and …er yes I'm sure we'll get on just fine.

WITCH: And you Rapunzel, Are you willing to marry this Beast?

RAPUNZEL: Well…er…if he becomes a little less Beastly, I suppose I must do what Daddy tells me.

WITCH: *(sarcastic)* If we all did what Daddy told us, what sort of lives would we lead?

RAPUNZEL: Nonetheless. It's been prophesied Auntie. I must fulfil my destiny.

WITCH: Right then. You lot. *(She turns to the audience)* This is one of the most difficult spells I have ever attempted. So sit right back in your seats or you might get hurt. Dim the lights! *(they dim)* Be prepared for a loud bang. Now I'm going to change the Beast back into what he used to be!

(Chants) All enchantments I dismiss
   When you have your *second* kiss

Kiss him again Rapunzel!

She does. There's a most impressive bang followed by a blackout. And then the lights come up again to reveal.... everything exactly the same as before

BEAST: Er….I'm still a Beast!

RAPUNZEL: Auntie Bertha?

ROYAL SOOTHSAYER: Your spell hasn't worked!

WITCH: It's worked perfectly. I've changed Gerald from what he was into what he is!

BEAST: But I'm still a Beast!

WITCH: You always were a Beast Gerald. You've never been under any enchantment! You were born a Beast. Your mother and father were Beasts. All this nonsense about you once being a handsome Prince is just that – nonsense.

ROYAL SOOTHSAYER: But my prophecy!

WITCH: That was nonsense as well. Like all of your prophecies.

BEAST: You mean -

WITCH: *(quite kindly)* Just be content with who you are Gerald. A big, manly, loveable hulk of a Beast.

ROYAL SOOTHSAYER: *(mocking)* Called Gerald!

BEAST: I enjoy being a Beast, you know!

WITCH: Of course you do. We should all enjoy being who we are – not who we want to be.

BEAST holds up placard saying "MORAL OF PLAY"

RAPUNZEL: But what about your spell Auntie? You must have done something. There was such a loud bang.

WITCH: My spell just now was a revealing spell. It's made you all realise what you really want in life – and who you really love.

Beat

WITCH: Go on think about it. Rapunzel?

Beat

RAPUNZEL: I love Jack. I'm sorry Mr Beast – I'm sure you're a very nice man, with a kind heart, but I've suddenly realised. I want to spend the rest of my life with Jack!

WITCH: What about you Gerald?

BEAST: I love you Bertha. I've suddenly realised. You're a wonderful, wonderful woman. I want to spend the rest of my life with you. I don't care that you're a Witch....

WITCH: *(with surprising tenderness)* And I don't care that you're a Beast....

Beat

ROYAL SOOTHSAYER: I love Rupert

ALL: Rupert?

ROYAL SOOTHSAYER: I want to spend the rest of my life with Rupert

BEAST: Rupert Bear?

RAPUNZEL: Who's Rupert

ROYAL SOOTHSAYER: Never you mind. I'm going off to tell him – now! (*and he does*)

BEAST: Well then! I think this calls for a celebratory drink, don't you? Stay there you two, and I'll go and get Jack to bring us some champagne *(He goes)*

RAPUNZEL: Oh Auntie Bertha! I'm so happy. I can't wait to see Jack!

WITCH: You won't have to wait too long dear. He's just changing into his costume.

KING: (*entering out of breath*) Ah. There you are! I've been looking everywhere for you! I'm not too late am I to get into this scene? I absolutely refuse to change the scenery this time.

RAPUNZEL: Don't worry Daddy. There's no scene-changing to do.

KING: Thank heavens for that!

RAPUNZEL: The play's almost finished.

KING: Finished! But that's not fair! I've hardly said a word since my bit in the Royal Throne Room!

RAPUNZEL: These good people have got homes to go to Daddy.

WITCH: Not for very long. They'll be tuna fish sandwiches in a few hours' time

RAPUNZEL :What?

WITCH: *(chuckles)* A little spell I put on them earlier in the play.

KING: You couldn't change them into muffins I suppose?

RAPUNZEL: Daddy, Daddy don't be so greedy! And Auntie Bertha – that's a horrid thing to do. I think to celebrate our good fortune, the least you can do is to remove the spell. *(to a little girl in the audience)* You don't want to be turned into a fish sandwich, do you? *("no")* There we are then.

WITCH: Oh very well! As it's a special day I'll take away the curse *(bang! And she does)* Think yourselves lucky, all of you! Very lucky!

KING: What's so special about today?

RAPUNZEL: *(seeing JACK enter with champagne)* I'm going to marry this man, Daddy!

KING: Oh – jolly good. You're the Beast I take it. Turned into a handsome Prince.

JACK: Actually I'm Jack.

KING: Jack? Strange name for a Prince, but beggars can't be choosers eh? Same for beasts I suppose. Still, you're a handsome fellow. Sorry about my daughter – she was more of a looker when she had hair, you know.

RAPUNZEL: Daddy!

KING: Her sister's the beauty in the family. Sheila.

RAPUNZEL: Shirley!

KING: Already taken I'm afraid.

JACK: I'm not the Beast Sire. I'm the Beast's manservant. Jack Robinson. The man who climbed the beanstalk.

KING: *(appalled)* What! That good for nothing rapscallion! You can't marry my daughter, you impudent young boy. You're a penniless nobody!

RAPUNZEL: Daddy! That's an awful thing to say!

KING: I never spoke a truer word. There's no way on earth I'm going to let you marry that wastrel!

WITCH: Horace – Horace - look into my eyes will you.

KING: *(surprised)* Oh – very well Bertha. What lovely eyes you have!

WITCH: All the better for seeing you my dear.... *(She clicks her fingers)*

KING: *(a bit confused)* Ah yes. Where was I? Oh yes I was just saying wasn't I, Jim, Jake, Jack – that it will be an absolute pleasure to welcome you into the Royal family – won't it Bertha?

WITCH: Indeed it will.

JACK: Thank you so much Sire. *(He takes RAPUNZEL'S hand)*

KING: Do you have any money?

JACK: Not a bean Sire.

KING: Oh – no matter! I've got plenty of money already.

JACK: Actually, come to think of it, I do have one bean left.

KING: Well – you can plant it in the Royal Vegetable Patch. I always enjoy a bean or two for lunch. That's when they become "has-beans"! *(laughs)* Geddit? Geddit? Good eh? Has-beens!

JACK: Very good Sire.

KING: My other daughter – Shelley - always used to laugh at that joke!

RAPUNZEL: Shirley!

KING: That's what I said. *(to a child)* Wasn't it? *("no")* No? You weren't listening properly. Wash your ears out! So - where's the Beast then?

JACK: He asked me to tell you all he'll be down shortly after the play's finished. He's just freshening up. Meantime he's invited us all to have a glass of champagne.

KING: Good, good. But before we do that, I think we should all sing a song, don't you? Anybody know any good songs?

JACK: There's the Hippopotamus song Sire.

KING: (I*n Scottish ROYAL SOOTHSAYER accent)* I know that one very well.

JACK: And we can ask the audience to join in with the Hippopotamuses.

KING: Excellent, excellent. Let's have some music then!

Song: The Hippopotamus Song (Reprise)

ROYAL SOOTHSAYER:
I feel such a silly clotamus, an awful idiotamus
Always finishing sentences by saying hippopotamus
It's such a silly word, and it's really quite absurd
I try hard not to say it, but I fear that I cannotamus....
Hippopotamus!

ALL JOIN IN FOR FOLLOWING VERSES:
Everywhere you go you hear an awful lot of rotamus
About the noble qualities this animal has gotamus.
He rolls around in mud, he's a thorough-going dud
An amazing smelly waste of space, a complete and absolute disgrace
Hippopotamus!

My favourite flower has always been the wild forgetmenotamus
My favourite living creature is the fearsome ocelotamus
But I couldn't give a fig, however small or big
For that ugly looking animal; I'd really like to ban 'em all
The Hippopotamus!

My favourite fruit, I'd like one now's, a juicy apricotamus
My favourite bird, lives by the sea's a lovely guillemotamus
But the creature we despise, it will come as no surprise
Is that good for nothing thimblerig, that dirty-looking jumped-up PIG...
AAHHGH! Hippopotamus!

He feels such a silly clotamus, an awful idiotamus
Always finishing sentences by saying hippopotamus
It's the creature we despise, it will come as no surprise
It's that good for nothing thimblerig, - that dirty-looking jumped-up pig
AAHHGH! Hippopotamus....
Oh Yeah!

KING: Well done everybody! Give yourselves a big round of applause! And an even bigger one for:

Princess Rapunzel *(They bow in turn)*

The Queen & The Witch

Jack and the Beast

And especially Me! The King & The Royal Soothsayer! The finest actor in the world!

Applause

KING: *(hushing the applause)* – And remember as you go out – a word of advice from someone who knows a bit about life. Never kiss a Beast if at all possible!

REST OF CAST: Hippopotamus!

CURTAIN

RUMPELSTILTSKIN AND THE SLEEPING BEAUTY

First performance at Colour House Theatre, Easter 2019

ORIGINAL CAST:

KING HORACE/ROYAL SOOTHSAYER/FAIRY GODMOTHER: Neil Summerville

PRINCE HOWARD/RUMPELSTILTSKIN: Sam Peterson

MELISSA/CINDERELLA: Lizzie Burder

QUEEN/WITCH: Sophia Lorenti

SCENES

SCENE 1 - The Royal Throne Room

SCENE 2 - The Royal Bedchamber

SCENE 3 - The Goblin's Hovel

SCENE 4 - The Wild Wood

SCENE 5 - The Goblin's Hovel

SCENE 6 - The Royal Drawing Room

SCENE 1 – THE ROYAL THRONE ROOM

The curtain opens to reveal KING HORACE, crown askew and legs dangling over an easy chair, munching his way through a rapidly diminishing pile of muffins. His face is streaked with butter and his shirt sleeves covered in jam. He seems surprised but unconcerned to find himself the centre of attention

KING: *(noticing the audience)* Ah – hello. Just having a muffin. You can't beat them you know. Some people prefer toasted teacakes of course – or hot buttered scones dripping with honey - but I've always been a muffin-man myself.

Fancy one little girl ? You do? Well sorry about that. I'm afraid there's none left! *(and indeed there aren't; the King has just shoved the last one into his mouth.)* Another time perhaps…

PRINCE HOWARD: *(entering, morosely* Hello Dad!

KING: What! Who are you? You can't come barging into the Royal Throne Room – I'll have your head cut off!

PRINCE: What are you taking about Dad! I'm your son – Howard!

KING: Ah yes – of course you are. I was forgetting I had a son. How are you Horace?

PRINCE: *You're* Horace! I'm Howard.

KING: That's what I said wasn't it? *(turns to audience for confirmation)* Wasn't it?

PRINCE: OK – Let's start again shall we. I'm Prince Howard; you're King Horace.

KING: I know perfectly well who I am, thank you Harry

PRINCE: Oh, what's the point….

KING: So what do you want anyway? Money? Muffins?

PRINCE: I just want some sympathy and understanding Dad. I'm in love. With a wonderful woman

KING: You're always in love with a wonderful woman. What's her name this week – Thumbelina? Pippi Longstocking? Or that wet little thing who has peas under her mattress?

PRINCE: You know perfectly well why she put peas under her -

KING: And please don't tell me she's another mermaid! The palace stank of fish for weeks after that last one. Your stepmother had to get a cleaning company in. Cost a fortune. (*start music*)

PRINCE: She's not a mermaid Dad.

KING: Thank the Lord for that

PRINCE: She's a sweet, simple country-girl . Her name is Cinderella. I met her at last night's ball. It was the best – and worst – night of my life. Let me tell you what happened – it's a very sad story.

Song: I'm In Love With Cinderella

PRINCE:
I'm just a simple fella

I'm in love with Cinderella

She's the only girl for me

CHORUS:
(Who dance in) She's the only girl…

PRINCE:
I tell you I will never meet

A girl so bright and clever

As you'll very shortly see

CHORUS :
She's the only girl…

PRINCE:
She's beautiful and funny

Though she hasn't got much money

But then again I've got enough for two

CHORUS:
He's loaded…

PRINCE:
We will live in bliss for ever

And I promise you I'll never

Meet a girl so good and true.

CHORUS:
So good and true…

PRINCE:
I met her at a ball
Which we held in our Grand Hall
And we danced the night away

CHORUS:
Danced the night away!

PRINCE:
But when the clock struck twelve

CHORUS:
Struck twelve

PRINCE:
She was quite beside herself

CHORUS:
Beside herself

PRINCE:
And cried loudly in dismay

CHORUS:
She cried loudly in dismay

PRINCE:
"Dear Prince I have to go
Even though I love you so"

CHORUS:
I love you so

PRINCE:
"I simply cannot stay"

CHORUS:
Simply cannot stay

PRINCE:
And with no intended malice
She rushed headlong from the palace
And disappeared… into the night

CHORUS:
She disappeared… into the night

PRINCE:
She left me no address
My life is now a mess

CHORUS:
His life's a mess

PRINCE:
What on earth am I to do?

CHORUS:
What on earth is he to do?

PRINCE:
But then on the ballroom floor
Just imagine what I saw
One delightful little shoe

CHORUS:
One delightful little shoe

PRINCE:
But on the ballroom floor

CHORUS:
On the ballroom floor

PRINCE:
Just imagine what I saw

CHORUS:
Guess what he saw

PRINCE & CHORUS:
One delightful little shoe

CHORUS:
One delightful little shoe

PRINCE:
(holding it up) One delightful little shoe!

CHORUS:
That's the end of our song.

And the Chorus dance off

KING: Sorry – let's just get this straight. She ran away from you as the clock struck midnight, and all you've got left to remind you of her is a "delightful little shoe"?

PRINCE: That's right Dad

KING: Don't you think her running away might be a bit of a give-away? It doesn't suggest she thought much of you. Rather the opposite in fact.

PRINCE: It was love at first sight Dad!

KING: Well with your track record you should know all about that...

PRINCE: She ran away because she was under some sort of spell. She wouldn't have left me otherwise.

KING: So how are you going to find her again?

PRINCE: Easy-peasy. I've got her shoe. I shall simply go round to every house in the kingdom until I find the foot that fits it. And that will be my Cinderella.

Beat

KING: Are you serious?

PRINCE: Of course I'm serious.

KING: Son...son. I know you're not the sharpest knife in the crayon box, but think about it for a moment, will you. This shoe is what – a size four?

PRINCE: Yes

KING: Well there must be at least five thousand girls in the kingdom who could slip into this!

PRINCE: So?

KING: You can't marry all of them.

Beat

PRINCE: Oh. I see what you mean. Bother! (*He tosses shoe into the wings*)

KING: My advice son – speaking as a man who knows a bit about life – is to look at her *face* next time. That's the way to remember 'em. Leave the feet to take care of themselves.

PRINCE: Thanks for that Dad

MELISSA, MISTRESS OF THE ROYAL BEDCHAMBER:
(extremely nervous) Excuse my me Liege...

KING: Who the hell are you? I'll have your head cut off….

PRINCE: Dad! Dad! Calm down. It's Melissa - Step-Mummy's personal maid. You've met her many times before…

KING: Ah yes, of course I have. Sorry! Sorry Meriam. What do you want?

MELISSA: *(struggling to remember her words)* It's the Queen Sire. She's very upset. She's creating quite a storm… *(FX storm)*

Consternation at this unexpected sound effect

PRINCE: *(out of character.)* It's Nathan. The techie we've employed. He's very enthusiastic but takes the script a bit literally.

KING: Oh for Heaven's sake! I'm getting soaked!

PRINCE: *(calling off)* Nathan! Turn it off please! *(He does)*

KING: So where were we?

MELISSA: I was just saying Sire. That it's the Queen, Sire! She's very upset. She's creating quite a storm… *(FX storm)*

KING/PRINCE: No Nathan! *(storm stops)*

MELISSA: She wants you to see Sire….

KING: Eh?

MELISSA: Sorry – I'm a bit nervous. It's my one big line in this scene you see ….

KING: Well say it then!

MELISSA: Er. *(to herself, quickly)* Excuse me my Liege…It's the Queen Sire. She's very upset. She's creating quite a…. storm… er…. …she wants to Sire you Sir… She wants you to see saw Sire…. no, no *(got it!)* She wants to see you Sire!

KING: *(a bit confused)* Right.

PRINCE: Where does she want to see him?

MELISSA: …In the Royal Bed?

KING: Ah – jolly good.

MELISSA: No, no – the Royal Bedchamber Sire. She's very bad Sire. Sad Sire.

PRINCE: Oh yes. She was telling me Dad. Some nasty business with a goblin.

KING: I wouldn't trust a goblin as far as I could throw him….. Right then. We'd better fly! *(FX aeroplane)* No, no techie bloke! It's a figure of speech for heaven's sake!

PRINCE: Nathan – this is a scene-change. Get ready for a blackout.

BLACKOUT

KING: No – not immediately. Not until we're off the stage you fool! Oh gobstoppers, I can't see a thing.

PRINCE: You can help change the scenery. *(He bumps into MELISSA)* Oops – sorry Melissa

MELISSA: *(coyly)* That's all right

PRINCE: A soft landing anyway! By the way – what size shoe do you take?

MELISSA: Er... size four I think.

PRINCE: Really….really….! Nathan, play some music will you?

MUSIC

SCENE 2 – THE ROYAL BEDCHAMBER

MELISSA: *(announcing)* The King to Sire you Madam….

QUEEN: What?!

MELISSA: To *see* you Madam…Sorry. Sorry Sire. *(the KING and PRINCE enter)*

KING: Hello my dear. Having a spot of bother with goblins I hear?

QUEEN: Oh Horace! You won't believe what's happened.

KING: Well not much point in telling me then.

QUEEN: It's too awful to talk about.

KING: Well let's not then. *(noticing baby)* Good Lord – what's that thing?

QUEEN: It's your son Horace!

KING: Nonsense – *my* name's Horace. And this chap here's my son. Aren't you Harry?

PRINCE: Howard!

KING: That's what I said. Wasn't it?

QUEEN: Howard is my *stepson* Horace. This is *our* child! Little Willie. Born yesterday afternoon, at half past four. Surely you haven't forgotten?

KING: Ah, yes of course. I remember. I was just tucking into a large plate of muffins – well, not the plate, obviously, just the muffins - when this girl of yours came and told me you'd had a child. Jolly well done my dear!

QUEEN: *(on point of tears)* It's not well done at all Horace! A goblin is coming to take him away.

KING: Now, now – don't cry darling. You'll have the baby crying next. *(FX baby cries)*

    (Calling off) No, no – that wasn't a cue you fool! Switch him off! *(he does)* Thank you. *(picks up baby)* Ah – little Wally.

QUEEN: Willie!

KING: Little Willie. Just like your father. Coochy, coochy, coo……Now - why not take him for a walk Meriam? *(He chucks the baby at her)*

MELISSA: Very Sire good. *(She leaves)*

QUEEN: *(cries again)*

PRINCE: Cheer up Step Mummy. It may never happen!

KING: What might never happen?

QUEEN: I can't tell you Horace!

KING: Well that's not much use, is it? These people here have paid good money to hear a ripping yarn, but if you can't be bothered to tell them, they might as well all toddle off home.

QUEEN: Howard knows! I've told *him*!

KING: So tell *me* then!

QUEEN: I can't. I'll act it out. It's less painful that way. You play the goblin for us Howard.

PRINCE: I'm not a very good actor.

KING: *(out of character)* You can say that again!

QUEEN: Don't be mean! You'll be fine as the goblin Howard. Wear that old green hat over there. It'll get you in character.

KING: Who are *you* playing?

QUEEN: The Queen, of course.

KING: But you *are* the Queen.

QUEEN: I'm playing myself as I was a year ago.

KING: *(confused)* Ah....

QUEEN: You remember when my father bought me to the palace and said I could spin gold from straw?

KING: Of course I do! That was the reason I married you.

QUEEN: And you locked me in a castle turret overnight, with a bundle of smelly old straw, and said that if I didn't spin every bit of straw into gold you'd have my head cut off?

KING: Gosh. Did I really?

PRINCE: Dad never meant it Step Mummy! He's always threatening to have people's heads cut off, but he never means it.

QUEEN: Yes, I know that *now* dear. But I didn't know it at the time. I thought this was going to be my last night on earth.

KING: But you did just fine. You spun all the straw into gold, and I was so pleased with you that I married you on the spot. My first wife having unfortunately perished after eating a poisoned apple...

PRINCE: Hazard of the job.

QUEEN: I never told you what *really* happened Horace. OK – imagine I've just been shut in a castle turret with nothing but straw and a spinning wheel to keep me company. *(She starts to act her younger self, with a very unconvincing American accent)* Oh help. What am I going to do?

KING: You're going to spin the straw into gold.

QUEEN: No, no – be quiet Horace. I'm acting out what happened. Oh help. What am I going to do?

Beat

PRINCE: Is that my cue?

QUEEN: Obviously.

PRINCE: *(bland)* Hello. I'm an unutterably evil goblin.

QUEEN: Nastier! Put some feeling into it!

PRINCE: *(from now on he becomes the character he will later play)* Hello. I'm an unutterably evil goblin.

QUEEN: Oh heavens! How did you get in here? The door's locked.

PRINCE: Simples. I magicked my way in. That's one of the best things about being unutterably evil. You can magic your way in anywhere.

QUEEN: Oh – woe is me! This is my last night on earth!

KING: Sorry, sorry. Hold on. You're playing yourself right?

QUEEN: Right.

KING: So why the American accent?

QUEEN: Because I'm acting Gwyneth Paltrow playing myself OK?

KING: *(confused)* Ah. Right

QUEEN: Oh – woe is me! This is my last night on earth!

PRINCE: *(unmoved)* Really? That's sad.

QUEEN: Unless I spin all this straw into gold, I'm going to have my head cut off.

PRINCE: So start spinning then.

QUEEN: You can't spin straw into gold!

PRINCE: I can!

QUEEN: Oh no you can't!

PRINCE: Oh yes I can

QUEEN: Oh no you can't!

PRINCE: Wanna bet?

QUEEN: Bet what?

PRINCE: OK, OK. Here's the deal. I spin this straw into gold – and you give me your first-born child!

QUEEN: But I haven't got a first-born child. I haven't got a child at all. I'm not even married!

PRINCE: You soon will be sweetheart! What King is going to turn down a woman who spins straw into gold eh? It's a no-brainer!

QUEEN: All right then. If I must. *(to KING in her own accent)* And he sat down at the loom and span all the straw into gold. And the look on your face when you came in the following morning!

KING: Yes – but wait a moment. You're telling me that this goblin fellow is going to come along and claim young Wotsit for himself?

QUEEN: *(close to tears again)* Yes. He's already been. He came round last night when you were asleep.

PRINCE: Hello Queenie!

KING: That's no way to address your Stepmother, son.

PRINCE: I'm the goblin, aren't I? I'm still acting.

KING: *(out of character)* You could have fooled me.

PRINCE: Hello Queenie! I've come for your first-born.

QUEEN: *(American again)* No, no – and a hundred times no!

PRINCE: I'm afraid you've got no choice Queenie. A deal's a deal. It's time to pay up.

QUEEN: Oh please Mr Goblin. You can't be as evil as you look.

PRINCE: Try me!

QUEEN: Take pity on a poor, defenceless woman.

PRINCE: You're not poor or defenceless! You're the Queen! You've got a whole army to protect you and you're the richest woman in the land.

QUEEN: That's not the point, is it? I'm a *mother*. This is my new-born son. I shall fight to the death to keep him.

PRINCE: Look. Don't be ridiculous! I'm an unutterably evil Goblin who could turn you into Marmite with a flick of my fingers.

QUEEN: Don't do that – I beg you!

PRINCE: But I tell you what. Despite being unutterably evil, I've got a kind heart. If you can guess my name I'll release you from your promise. I can't say fairer than that.

QUEEN: Your name?

PRINCE: I'll give you three guesses. And you don't have to make them now, or the play will finish far too quickly.

QUEEN: Ah…

PRINCE: I'll be back in precisely 24 hours, and you can make them then. It'll give you time to get to know your baby before you hand him over to me! Ha ha ha!!!

QUEEN: *(normal accent)* And with that he vanished. Before I even had time to ask him what his name was.

KING: Yes – that would have helped. *(turns to PRINCE)* What *is* your name?

PRINCE: Howard!

KING: There we are! Problem solved my dear. The goblin's name is Howard.

PRINCE: I'm not the goblin anymore Dad! Howard's *my* name. I doubt very much it's the goblin's.

KING: Mmm…. Well this looks like a job for my brother, don't you think? The Royal Soothsayer.

QUEEN: Tiresias?!

KING: He's meant to know things. I wonder what's he like on goblins' names?

QUEEN: The man's a useless layabout Horace. We only keep him on because he's your brother.

KING: Give him a chance. He's got to strike lucky sometime. And perhaps he can help you find your umbrella woman son?

PRINCE: Cinderella!

KING: That's what I said, wasn't it? Right we haven't got a minute to lose. Footprints on the sands of time are not made by sitting down…

PRINCE/QUEEN: What?!

KING: We must fly *(FX aeroplane)*

PRINCE: No, no Nathan! Just give us a blackout! *(Blackout)*

KING: Honestly! Where did they find him!

QUEEN: Stop talking and shift the furniture Horace.

KING: Ow! *(He's tripped over)* I'm the King. I'm not paid to shift the furniture! Play some music somebody!

And somebody does just that

SCENE 3 – THE GOBLIN'S HOVEL

Lights go up to reveal CINDERELLA (initially apparently asleep but opens her eyes and shows she isn't)

CINDERELLA: Oh hello everybody. How lovely to see you. What are your names. Shout them out to me (*audience does so*) Louder than that! I think I missed a couple. (*louder audience*) Jolly good! Heather! (*choosing a name she's just heard*) What a lovely name. I had a budgie called Heather. He was eaten by our cat. It was very sad. Feathers all over the place.

Anyway, can you guess who I am? Any ideas anyone? *(audience: "Cinderella")*

Yes – well done you! I'm Cinderella. And I'm trapped here in an evil goblin's hovel. You haven't seen him have you? He wears a dirty green hat.

Well look. I need your help. If you do see him please warn me by booing very loudly. That way I can jump into bed and pretend to be asleep. I feel safer there. Shall we have a practice? I'll pretend to be the goblin – Right here I come – you boo me, OK?

(Boos)

That's good but not good enough. *Really loudly now*! OK – let's try again…

(Boos)

Much better! Much better! I feel a lot safer now. But I'm still very unhappy. Let me explain: (*fx music*)

Song: I'm So Sad

          CHORUS:
(Comes in singing) She's so sad
Oh so sad
She's so sad
Oh so sad.

      CINDERELLA:
I'm so sad
I'm so sad

Imprisoned in a hovel
The experience is quite novel
But the outlook is quite bad

CHORUS:
….quite bad

CINDERELLA:
What to do?
What to do?
I'm the victim of a spell
Staying here's a living hell
And I've only got one shoe

CHORUS:
….one shoe

CINDERELLA:
I just hope
I just hope
That the Prince will not upset me
If he doesn't come and get me
I just know that I won't cope

CHORUS:
… won't cope

CINDERELLA:
He is brave!
He's so brave
But unless he sets me free
Comes along and rescues me
I shall be the Goblin's slave

CHORUS:
…his slave

CINDERELLA:
He's unutterably evil
As cunning as a weevil
He's the most malicious fella
Obsessed with Cinderella
But if I'm forced to stay

If I fail to get away
It's the end for Cinderella
It's the end

CHORUS:
(*Dancing off*) It's the end…. for Cinderella
It's the end…. for Cinderella
It's the end…. for Cinderella

CINDERELLA:
It's the end…. for Cinderella

CINDERELLA: Oh dear….I feel so depressed. *(goes to sit on bed)* I'm locked in this hovel, I'm all alone and I haven't got a friend in the world.

There's a magic sting and the FAIRY GODMOTHER suddenly appears.

FAIRY GODMOTHER: Hello sweetie!

CINDERELLA: Who are you!?

FAIRY GODMOTHER: You remember me dear! I arranged for you to go the ball last night. I'm Titania - your Fairy Godmother.

CINDERELLA: I can see you're a fairy. But I don't remember having any godmother.

FAIRY GODMOTHER: You're too young to remember sweetie. Oooh…do you mind . My feet are killing me! Shift up will you. (*He gets on the bed with her*)

CINDERELLA: What are you doing here?

FAIRY GODMOTHER: What are *you* doing here, more to the point? Don't you know this is an evil goblin's hovel?

CINDERELLA: Of course I know. I've been kidnapped haven't I?

FAIRY GODMOTHER: Who by?

CINDERELLA: The goblin, of course! (GETS UP) I was rushing out of the Palace last night to get my coach, and this horrible goblin tapped me on the shoulder and said:

Fx evil sting

RUMPELSTILTSKIN: (*magically appears*) Looking for something darling?

CINDERELLA: Er…yes….I was looking for my coach actually.

RUMP: There's no coach here love, There's a large pumpkin over there, if that's any use.

CINDERELLA: Oh no! It must be past midnight!

RUMPELSTILTSKIN: Way past! It's been tomorrow for ages.

CINDERELLA: But how am I going to get home? My sisters will kill me if I'm late.

RUMPELSTILTSKIN: You've got sisters eh? Are they lookers like you? Any pics?

CINDERELLA: Well…yes…you can have a look on my iPhone if you like (S*he shows him*)

RUMPELSTILTSKIN: (*horrified*) O.M.G. they're ugly!

CINDERELLA: You wouldn't dare say that to their faces.

RUMPELSTILTSKIN: I'm an unutterably evil goblin honey! I can say anything I like to anybody!

CINDERELLA: What am I going to do?!

RUMPELSTILTSKIN: Well – I'll give you three options. You could stay here in your party frock and freeze to death.

CINDERELLA: Next?

RUMPELSTILTSKIN: Or you could try walking home, but it's the middle of the night, you've no idea where you are, and you've only got one shoe on.

CINDERELLA: I've got a feeling I'm going to plump for option three….

RUMPELSTILTSKIN: Or you could let *me* take you home love. You'll be perfectly safe with me – even though I am an unutterably evil goblin.

CINDERELLA: I don't really have much choice, do I?

RUMPELSTILTSKIN: 'Fraid not Hun. Hop into this pumpkin then, and off we go….

CINDERELLA: At which point he changed the pumpkin into a quad bike and drove me here. (*FX quad bike - rather longer than necessary*) OK, OK – Thanks Nathan!

Then he locked me in this room, put a spell on the door, and said he was going off to get me a baby.

FAIRY GODMOTHER: That's an unusual way to go about it....

CINDERELLA: Oh Fairy Godmother! What am I going to do?! Can you get me out of here?

FAIRY GODMOTHER: I'm sorry my dear, but I'm afraid I can't. A Goblin's magic is stronger than mine. He's put an enchantment on this room, and the only way to release you from it is with a kiss.

CINDERELLA: Then kiss me. I don't mind. I won't report you.

FAIRY GODMOTHER: *I'm* not kissing you darling. Fairies' kisses won't work. You have to be kissed by a handsome Prince! You don't happen to know any I suppose?

CINDERELLA: I do actually. His name's Howard. He's the most handsome Prince in the world. And I'm in love with him.

FAIRY GODMOTHER: Well you won't mind being kissed by him then, will you?

CINDERELLA: Bring it on! But how will he find me?

FAIRY GODMOTHER: Leave that to me dear. The Royal Soothsayer is a good friend of mine. I'll tell him that you need to be rescued and get him to bring your Howard with him.

CINDERELLA: Oh Fairy Godmother, how can I ever thank you!

FAIRY GODMOTHER: Just give us a kiss. (*Cinderella obliges*) That's nice. Now dear – I must be going. The goblin will be back any moment.

CINDERELLA: (*fearful*) How do you know?

FAIRY GODMOTHER: It's in the script. Haven't you read it? We've only got two more speeches.

CINDERELLA: I'd better pretend to be asleep.

FAIRY GODMOTHER: And I'd better go. Those were the two speeches. Good luck ducky! *(She goes)*

Beat

FX: evil sting

RUMPELSTILTSKIN enters to much booing

RUMPELSTILTSKIN: *(to audience)* Don't you boo me you pathetic blobs of humanity. I'm surprised they let you in. You're the ugliest audience we've had this week. *(to an audience member)* But you look a nice little girl dear... Would you like a goblin for a friend? You could be my servant and cook for me. Any good at cooking? No? Well that's hopeless. Luckily I've found myself a nice lady.. Look – there she is – fast asleep in the bed. Isn't she lovely eh? The Sleeping Beauty, that's what I'll call her. And she's all mine! And I'm bringing home a baby for her – the Queen's first born. We'll be one big happy family!! Ha ha ha! The Queen's only chance of keeping her baby is to guess my name – and she'll never do that. *Nobody* knows my name! *(to the audience)* What are you laughing at? You haven't the faintest idea what my name is, have you? *(somebody will call it out)* What! What! How on earth did you know that? You read it on the poster outside the theatre didn't you! I told that fool of a director not to print it. And don't you dare tell the Queen, or I'll turn you all into jam doughnuts OK? I will. I will. I'm an unutterably evil Goblin, and I do things like that all the time. So watch it!

(He turns to CINDERELLA) Ah my dear, sweet sleeping beauty. Are you dreaming about me? About the wonderful life we're going to have together? You, me and the Queen's new baby? Wow - I feel quite teary just thinking about it. I must get back to being unutterably evil... Nathan! Give me a blast of lightning! *(FX lightning)* And some Thunder! *(FX thunder)* Right – I'm off to the Palace to claim the baby. Evil Music please!

BLACKOUT & EVIL MUSIC

SCENE 4 – THE WILD WOOD

WITCH: (*approaches and looks disapprovingly at audience*) What are you lot doing here? I wasn't expecting to see *you*. What an ugly-looking bunch you are! You'd be much better off as tuna-fish sandwiches don't you think? I'm very good at turning people into tuna-fish sandwiches; it's a speciality of mine. Now then - is there a Sally here? (*choose name of a known audience member*) Tell me Sally, do you like your tuna-fish sandwiches made with brown bread or white?

If she says brown: Brown? I bet your Mummy's told you that's healthier, hasn't she? And of course she's right. Give me a wholemeal or Granary tuna fish sandwich any day. Don't you worry – if I have to turn you into a tuna-fish sandwich – and I hope I won't have to - I'll make sure you're best quality brown bread.

If she says white: White! What an appalling choice! White bread tastes like a cardboard box that's been left out in the rain. Haven't you been taught anything? Well don't you worry – if I have to turn you into a tuna-fish sandwich – and I hope I won't have to - I'll make sure you're best quality *brown* bread. Wholemeal – or possibly Granary.

Now I'm looking for my nephew, Prince Howard. He's fallen in love again – he's always falling in love – but this time he thinks he's on to a winner. She's called Cinderella and I understand she's been captured and locked in a hovel by an utterably evil goblin. But I can help him find her! I can break that wicked goblin's spell, with a bolt of lightning from my wand! (*fx lightning bolt*) No. no not now Nathan - wait until I do the actual spell! ! (*going*) Honestly- the boy's an idiot.......

(*She leaves stage right – from left comes the ROYAL SOOTHSAYER and PRINCE*)

ROYAL SOOTHSAYER: This way Prince – Hippopotamus - Woof

PRINCE: Pardon?

ROYAL: SOOTHSAYER Hippopotamus – Woof. I'm so sorry Prince. Hippopotamus –Woof

PRINCE: Are you feeling all right Dad?

ROYAL SOOTHSAYER: I'm not your Dad - I'm the Royal Soothsayer!

PRINCE: Oh of course. Yes. You're his twin brother. That's why you look so like him. I just get confused sometimes.

ROYAL SOOTHSAYER: *(unimpressed by the speech)* Born five minutes after the King, and to stop any confusion sent to live for thirty-seven years with our Aunty Jean in Glasgow, which explains my Scottish accent.

PRINCE: *(out of character)* Who wrote that line? It's garbage!

ROYAL SOOTHSAYER: Precisely - Hippopotamus! Woof!

PRINCE: Er....

ROYAL: SOOTHSAYER It's that's darned Witch, Prince - Hippopotamus Woof! I can't *bear* her! Woof. She's cursed me again.

PRINCE: Oh yes – I remember – when my elder sister Shirley got married, she cursed you, and you used to bark every time an animal was mentioned. Like dog

ROYAL SOOTHSAYER: Woof.

PRINCE: Or cat.

ROYAL SOOTHSAYER: Woof!

PRINCE: And when my younger sister Rapunzel got married you used to say Hippopotamus -

ROYAL SOOTHSAYER: Woof!

PRINCE: - every time someone said a word beginning with 'P'

ROYAL SOOTHSAYER: Hippopotamus! Woof!

PRINCE: So it's happened again?

ROYAL SOOTHSAYER: Precisely. Hippopotamus. Woof! And it's double bubble this time. She's cursed me twice over – and all for accidentally locking her out of the castle one night.

PRINCE: What a cow!

ROYAL SOOTHSAYER: Woof!

PRINCE: Sorry – sorry – I'll try not to mention any animals.

ROYAL SOOTHSAYER: And words beginning with.....the letter after "O"

PRINCE: "P".

ROYAL SOOTHSAYER: Hippopotamus! Woof!

PRINCE: Sorry. Sorry…. No animals. No words beginning with "P."

ROYAL SOOTHSAYER: Hippopotamus! Woof!

PRINCE: Precisely.

ROYAL SOOTHSAYER: Hippopotamus! Woof!

PRINCE: But why do you woof as well as saying hippopotamus?

ROYAL SOOTHSAYER: Woof. Because it's an animal, isn't it?

PRINCE: Hippopotamus?

ROYAL SOOTHSAYER: Woof.

PRINCE: Ah. Gotcha.

Pause

PRINCE: Anyway. Where exactly are we? Do you know?

ROYAL SOOTHSAYER: Er. Not exactly your Royal Highness. Titania told me that that nice young lady you met at the ball -

PRINCE: Cinderella -

ROYAL SOOTHSAYER: Cinderella had been kidnapped by an unutterably evil goblin and was trapped in a hovel deep in the heart of the Wild Wood.

PRINCE: Well we're deep in the heart of the Wild Wood now aren't we?

ROYAL SOOTHSAYER: Possibly. Hippopotamus! Woof. But I don't see any hovel.

PRINCE: Hovels aren't always easy to spot. That's the thing about hovels. One minute you won't see any, and the next they're all over the place.

ROYAL SOOTHSAYER: Hippopotamus! Woof.

MELISSA: *(appears totally unexpectedly)* There's a goblin to see you Sire.

ROYAL SOOTHSAYER /PRINCE: (*taken aback*) What?!!

MELISSA: There's a goblin to -

PRINCE: Melissa? What are you doing here? You're not in this scene.

MELISSA: Aren't I? I thought that was my cue. "Hippopotamus Woof."

ROYAL SOOTHSAYER: Woof!

MELISSA: Pardon?

ROYAL SOOTHSAYER: Hippopotamus! Woof!

MELISSA: There's a goblin to see you Sire.

PRINCE: No! No Melissa! You say that to my father in two scenes' time!

ROYAL SOOTHSAYER: There's no goblin *here* is there you silly woman! Or any King for that matter.

MELISSA: I thought you were the King.

ROYAL SOOTHSAYER: I'm his twin brother!

MELISSA: You look awful. Like him.

ROYAL SOOTHSAYER: *(surprised)* Eh?

PRINCE: *(kindly, sotto voce)* No, no Melissa. The line you're meant to say is "You look awfully like him."

MELISSA: Sorry. Sorry. You look awfully like him.

ROYAL SOOTHSAYER: That's the thing about twins! They tend to look awfully like each other.

PRINCE: Precisely!

ROYAL SOOTHSAYER: Hippopotamus! Woof!

MELISSA: There's a goblin to see you Sire.

ROYAL SOOTHSAYER: *(irritated)* No no!

PRINCE: *(kindly)* Melissa. Believe me. You say that line in two scenes' time. When there actually IS a goblin to see the King.. OK?

MELISSA: I'm sorry Prince

ROYAL SOOTHSAYER: Hippopotamus! Woof.

MELISSA: There's a goblin to see you Sire.

ROYAL SOOTHSAYER /PRINCE: *No, no!*

MELISSA: *(confused)* Sorry...sorry...there *isn't* a goblin to see you Sire.

PRINCE: That's right Melissa. Well done!

Beat

MELISSA: (*confused*) I'll go now shall I?

PRINCE: Please.

ROYAL SOOTHSAYER: Hippopotamus! Woof!

MELISSA: There's a goblin to see you Sire.

PRINCE: No! No goblins. Nobody! And you're going back off to the Palace

ROYAL SOOTHSAYER: Hippopotamus! Woof!

MELISSA: *(completely confused)* There's a goblin to see you Sire. Possibly?

ROYAL SOOTHSAYER: Hippopotamus! Woof!

MELISSA: There's a goblin to see you Sire

PRINCE: Melissa! Please!

ROYAL SOOTHSAYER: Hippopotamus! Woof!

MELISSA: (*can't stop herself now*) There's a goblin to….

ROYAL SOOTHSAYER: *(completely losing it)* JUST GO WOMAN! OK!

MELISSA: *(hurt - going)* All right I'm going. I'm going. *(hurt)* There's no need to shout Prince.

ROYAL SOOTHSAYER: *(exhausted)* Hippopotamus! Woof! Where did they find her?!

PRINCE: She's somebody's niece I believe…..Right then. We'd better continue our hovel-hunt. I want to find out what that unutterably evil goblin is doing to my Cinderella. It doesn't bear thinking about...

ROYAL SOOTHSAYER: Woof!

PRINCE: What?

ROYAL SOOTHSAYER: You said "bear". Woof.

PRINCE: Sorry. Anyway - Come on! *(calls out)* Cinderella! Don't despair! We'll rescue you! Tiresias – follow me - this looks a likely path.

ROYAL SOOTHSAYER: Hippopotamus! Woof!

They leave as the WITCH enters from the opposite

WITCH: Oh. It's you again. Has anybody seen Prince Howard? When? Where did he go? *(ad lib appropriately)* This way? Right – I'll follow him. But look – before I go, how would you like to hear my song? Not at all, or *very much*? Eh? Eh? Don't be shy. Though I should warn you that anybody who says "not at all" gets turned into a tuna-fish sandwich immediately. On *white* bread!

Good. Everyone wants to hear it then. So it would be a shame to disappoint you... Music Nathan - get on with it!

Witch's Song

WITCH:
You don't get rich
Being a Witch....
But it's fun.
You don't get rich
Being a Witch.
For if I give my wand a twirl
I can turn you little girl
Into a scrumptious currant bun.
O yes I could – perhaps I should
Get on my broom ,
Fly round this room
And make a chicken casserole of
Everyone....

But don't despair.
I'm very fair ask anyone.
But don't despair.
I'm very fair
If you treat me with respect,
Admire my fearsome intellect,
Then we'll have fun.

> In retrospect
> We'll have a ball.
> But if you make me hopping mad
> I can be very, very bad
> Turn your fingers into butter,
> Throw your toys into the gutter,
> Every one...
>
> Every Witch
> Must have a cat
> I can't -

RUMPELSTILTSKIN: *(suddenly arriving and cutting her off mid flow)* In the name of all that's evil will you stop that appalling racket! There are people here trying to sleep you know. *(He waves vacantly at audience)*

WITCH: How dare you stop me in the middle of my song – I've got three more verses to go!

RUMPELSTILTSKIN: Well you can sing 'em somewhere else!

WITCH: Do you know who I am??

RUMPELSTILTSKIN: Some old lady down on her luck? I've seen better gear on a scarecrow.

WITCH: I'm the Wicked Witch of West Wimbledon!

RUMPELSTILTSKIN: Well bully for you! I'm an unutterably evil goblin, but I don't make a song and dance of it.

WITCH: Ah! So it's you!

RUMPELSTILTSKIN: Well I don't see anybody else here, do you darling?

WITCH: Don't you darling me....

RUMPELSTILTSKIN: I'll do exactly what I like. Where's the fun in being unutterably evil, if you can't say exactly what you want, to whom you want, when you want?

WITCH: I warn you, I'm *much* wickeder than you!

RUMPELSTILTSKIN: Rubbish! You haven't the faintest idea how wicked I am.

WITCH: You're a nasty little goblin!

RUMPELSTILTSKIN: You don't even know my name.

WITCH: It's Rumpelstiltskin.

RUMPELSTILTSKIN: What! What! How did you know that? Nobody knows my name!

WITCH: It's plastered all over the theatre you stupid goblin.

RUMPELSTILTSKIN: Well don't you go telling the Queen!

WITCH: Why on earth would I tell the Queen?

RUMPELSTILTSKIN: Good, good. Anyway – as this audience knows, I'm much more wicked than you.

WITCH: Nonsense. I've just threatened to turn them all into tuna-fish sandwiches. They know *I'm* the really wicked one.

RUMPELSTILTSKIN: Nonsense! (*Music starts*) Listen to this Witchy. You can't argue with this....

Song: There's No One Quite So Wicked...

RUMPELSTILTSKIN:
A goblin is as wicked, he's as wicked as can be
I'm always doing wicked things for everyone to see
I put salt in people's sugar, I put marmite in their tea
No there's no one quite so wicked, quite so wicked as is me

CHORUS:
(Everyone else) Wicked! Wicked! Wicked!
A goblin is as wicked, he's as wicked as can be
He's always doing wicked things for everyone to see
He puts salt in people's sugar, he puts marmite in their tea
No there's no one quite so wicked, quite so wicked as is he
Wicked! Wicked! Wicked!

WITCH:
You tell me that you're wicked. Well I find that really rich
I could magic all your clothes away and chuck you in a ditch
I could bring you out in boils and make your ear-lobes itch
No there's no one quite so wicked, quite so wicked as a witch

CHORUS:
Wicked! Wicked!
He tells her that he's wicked. Well she finds that really rich
She could magic all his clothes away and chuck him in a ditch
She could bring him out in boils and make his ear-lobes itch
No there's no one quite so wicked, quite so wicked as a witch.
Wicked! Wicked!

RUMPELSTILTSKIN:
I'm full of wicked projects, I'm as busy as a bee

WITCH:
I could grab all your possessions and then chuck 'em in the sea

RUMPELSTILTSKIN:
I could cook you for my lunch

WITCH:
And I could eat you for my tea

BOTH:
No there's no one quite so wicked, quite so wicked as is me

CHORUS:
Wicked! Wicked! Wicked!

RUMPELSTILTSKIN:
I could turn your scrawny cat into a smelly kangaroo

WITCH:
I could kick your ugly goblin's hat from here to Timbuktu

RUMPELSTILTSKIN:
I could turn you into butter

WITCH:
I could boil you in a stew

BOTH:
But there's no one quite so goody good, so goody good as **you!**

CHORUS:
(Dancing off) Bye!

RUMPELSTILTSKIN: Goody-good? That's the very *last* thing I am Witch. But if you don't believe me, let's ask the audience shall we? *(to audience)* Right – When I count to three, I want you all to shout "Goblin" if you think I'm the wickeder.

RUMPELSTILTSKIN

WITCH: And if you think I am, I want you all to shout "Witch"!

RUMPELSTILTSKIN: One – two – three - *go*! *(the audience shout)*

WITCH: Louder. Come on, louder! *(the audience shout louder)*

RUMPELSTILTSKIN: A resounding victory for the goblin! Even you can't deny that!

WITCH: *(if Goblin does win)* That's only because they're one of the stupidest audiences we've ever had…

(If equal booing or Witch the winner) You need to get your hearing aid adjusted Rumpelstiltskin. I won easily!

RUMPELSTILTSKIN: Go on - tell me one recent wicked thing you've done?

WITCH: The Royal Soothsayer – you know the bloke?

RUMPELSTILTSKIN: The old git with the dodgy Scottish accent?

WITCH: That's the one.

RUMPELSTILTSKIN: Twin brother of the King?

WITCH: Because of me he ends up saying nothing but "Hippopotamus Woof!"

MELISSA: *(appearing)* There's a goblin to see you Sire!

WITCH/RUMPELSTILTSKIN: *(both seem to be expecting this)* Go away!

MELISSA: *(quickly going)* Sorry! Sorry!

WITCH: Stupid girl! Where was I? Ah yes. I was telling you about the curse I've put on the Royal Soothsayer.

RUMPELSTILTSKIN: That *is* wicked – I'll give you that.

WITCH: Thanks. Perhaps a little *too* wicked actually. I think I'll take away the "woofing" spell. *(FX: spell)* There. That should do it.

RUMPELSTILTSKIN: You'll never guess what I've done!

WITCH: You've kidnapped Cinderella and imprisoned her in your dirty little hovel.

RUMPELSTILTSKIN: How did you know that? How did you know that? They told you, didn't they! *(points to audience)*. I never liked the look of them. Ugly lot – especially the adults.

WITCH: Never you mind who told me. I'm going to put a stop to it.

RUMPELSTILTSKIN: You mind your own business Witchy, or I'll turn your broom into a donkey

FX donkey braying

RUMPELSTILTSKIN: and WITCH No Nathan!

WITCH: *(out of character)* There's a donkey for you!

RUMPELSTILTSKIN: Well - I'm off to the Queen now to get her little baby. He'll come and live with me and my Sleeping Beauty. We'll be one big happy family and I'll never have to be wicked again.

WITCH: In your dreams goblin!

RUMPELSTILTSKIN: You just wait and see Witch! My magic is more powerful than yours. There's nothing you can do to stop me

WITCH: Well we'll see about that....

RUMPELSTILTSKIN: Toodleoo sweetie! Mind how you fly! *(he goes)*

Beat

WITCH: I think I know how to defeat him. *(to audience)* It's up to you, actually. He's going to ask the Queen to guess his name, but she won't have a clue. You're going to have to tell her. But listen – this is dangerous work – there's every possibility he might turn you all into jam doughnuts in revenge. He does that sort of thing. Would you like that? *(audience reply)*

No...I should think not. But don't worry. Be brave! *(fx spell)* There – I've put a spell on him which will stop him doing this. But it will only work if you wait until the Queen asks you what his name is. You mustn't tell her *before* she asks. Got that? Let's have a practice. I'll be the Queen. I'm quite good at her.

"Tell me audience. Does anybody know the Goblin's name?"

(Audience: Rumpelstiltskin!)

Come on – louder than that. And it's Rumpelstiltskin, not RumpleSILKskin. OK – wait for it...."Does anybody know the Goblin's name?"

(Audience: Rumpelstiltskin!)

Good, good – that's better. But remember – *wait until she asks you!* Don't tell her before she does, or you'll ruin everything. The whole fate of the Royal Family depends on you!

BEAT

Good luck!

BLACKOUT & MUSIC

SCENE 5 – THE GOBLIN'S HOVEL

The ROYAL SOOTHSAYER and PRINCE are outside; CINDERELLA inside.

ROYAL SOOTHSAYER: *(calling)* Hello? Anybody there?

CINDERELLA: Yes! I am!

PRINCE: Oh my! I'd recognise that voice anywhere.

CINDERELLA: Who's that?

PRINCE: Cinderella! It's me, I've come to rescue you.

CINDERELLA: Who's me?

PRINCE: *(a bit put out)* Your Prince!

ROYAL SOOTHSAYER: Hippopotamus!

CINDERELLA: Pardon?

ROYAL SOOTHSAYER: Hippopotamus

CINDERELLA: You're a Hippopotamus?

PRINCE: No darling, it's Prince Howard!

ROYAL SOOTHSAYER: Hippopotamus

PRINCE: *(to ROYAL SOOTHSAYER)* You've stopped woofing.

ROYAL SOOTHSAYER: I know! Wonderful isn't it. Bear! Fox! Mongoose! I can say them all without barking.

PRINCE: Panther?

ROYAL SOOTHSAYER: Hippopotamus..

PRINCE: Pelican?

ROYAL SOOTHSAYER: Hippopotamus

PRINCE: Parrot?

ROYAL SOOTHSAYER: Hippopotamus.

PRINCE: Not a *total* success then?

ROYAL SOOTHSAYER: Yes, but that's because they all begin with the letter P! Hippopotamus!

PRINCE: Oh I see. You mean the only reason that you're saying -

CINDERELLA: *(a bit put out by this diversion)* I say – sorry to

RUMPELSTILTSKIN

interrupt you both – but did you say you'd come to rescue me?

PRINCE: Oh - Yes my darling.

CINDERELLA: And you really are my Prince?

ROYAL SOOTHSAYER: Hippopotamus.

PRINCE: I am, my darling.

CINDERELLA: Did you bring my shoe?

PRINCE: *(surprised at the question)* Er. No. Sorry about that.

CINDERELLA: It was a Jimmy Choo!

PRINCE: I'm sure Jimmy's got other shoes darling. I'll buy you hundreds when we marry.

CINDERELLA: Then come in and rescue me my Prince!

ROYAL SOOTHSAYER: Hippopotamus!

PRINCE: Here I come my darling! *(FX: electrical woosh as the PRINCE attempts to enter. He jumps back)* Er…sorry….bit of a problem.

ROYAL SOOTHSAYER: Hippopotamus.

PRINCE: I don't seem to be able to get through to you.

ROYAL SOOTHSAYER: Leave it to me Prince…Hippopotamus. *(FX: electrical woosh as he too tries and fails to enter)*

PRINCE: Let me try running at it very hard…… *(He does so, there's another whoosh and he bounces off thin air and lands in a heap)*

ROYAL SOOTHSAYER: Are you all right Prince…Hippopotamus?

PRINCE: *(dusting himself down)* Er…yes…I think so. No important bits broken. Hopefully.

ROYAL SOOTHSAYER: I say – Cinderella – why don't *you* come out to *us*? That'll save us coming in to you.

CINDERELLA: I wish I could, but I can't! The goblin has put a forcefield all round his hovel, and nobody but him can get in or out. That's why I haven't been able to escape.

PRINCE: Oh bother!

ROYAL SOOTHSAYER: *(reproachfully)* You could have told us!

PRINCE: It does leave us in a bit of a pickle.

ROYAL SOOTHSAYER: Hippopotamus

PRINCE: Oh do be quiet!

ROYAL SOOTHSAYER: Sorry Prince…Hippopotamus.

PRINCE: Stop hippopotamising and help us get rid of this spell.

ROYAL SOOTHSAYER: I don't do spells my Liege. That's not my forte. I'm the Royal Soothsayer.

CINDERELLA: What's a Soothsayer?

ROYAL SOOTHSAYER: *(proudly)* Somebody who says sooths. Somebody who looks into the future and tells you what's going to happen.

CINDERELLA: So what's going to happen now?

ROYAL SOOTHSAYER: I've no idea.

PRINCE: You're useless!

ROYAL SOOTHSAYER: That's a little harsh Sire.

PRINCE: I wish my Auntie Bertha was here; she'd know what to do.

FX: a flash of lightning

WITCH: You called Howard?

ROYAL SOOTHSAYER: Oh Lord, it's you…..

PRINCE: Auntie! How lovely to see you! We've got a problem..

ROYAL SOOTHSAYER: Hippopotamus!

WITCH: Oh hello … You particularly poisonous person *(emphasising "p's")*

ROYAL SOOTHSAYER: Hippopotamus, hippopotamus, hippopotamus

WITCH: How satisfying to see a spell of mine working so well Precious.

ROYAL SOOTHSAYER: *(sourly)* Hippopotamus

PRINCE: Auntie, auntie – can you help us? We need to break the unutterably evil goblin's spell and rescue my beautiful Cinderella.

RUMPELSTILTSKIN

WITCH: Well she's better-looking than her sisters, I'll give you that.

CINDERELLA: Thanks very much.....

WITCH: But I rather liked that girl you rescued from the bears' house. What was her name? Goldylicks?

PRINCE: Goldi*locks*! Not up to the mark I'm afraid. She was always wolfing porridge

ROYAL SOOTHSAYER : Hippopotamus!

PRINCE: and sleeping in strangers' beds...

ROYAL SOOTHSAYER: Yuk!

PRINCE: No, no Auntie, Cinderella is the only woman for me!

WITCH: Very well – I'll see if I can help. Now we must do this by the book. You dear, lie down over there and go to sleep.

CINDERELLA: But I don't feel at all sleepy!

FX: spell

WITCH: Well you do now.

CINDERELLA: *(yawns)* Oh - I'm *so* tired...... *(She falls down on her bed and goes into a deep sleep)*

PRINCE: *(appalled)* You've killed her Auntie!

WITCH: Not at all dear. She's just having forty winks. Now It's your task Howard, to wake her with a kiss, marry her, and live happily ever after.

PRINCE: That's all very well. But I can't get into the hovel!

FX: spell sting

WITCH: You can now dear!

PRINCE: *(steps into the hovel)* You're right! I can! Oh thank you *so* much Auntie.

WITCH: Always happy to help Howard. *(waves broomstick)* Now forgive me - I must fly!

PRINCE: Aren't you going to stay and watch me kiss her?

WITCH: No – I've got a costume-change to make. See you later dear. *(to ROYAL SOOTHSAYER)* Oh – and goodbye Precious!

ROYAL SOOTHSAYER: *(sulky)* Hippopotamus! *(the WITCH flies off)*

BEAT

PRINCE: Right! Wish me luck Tiresias! (*He goes over to bed and looks lovingly at her*)

ROYAL SOOTHSAYER: Well go on – kiss her then!

PRINCE: Shouldn't I ask her permission first?

ROYAL SOOTHSAYER: Hippopotamus! Don't be ridiculous – she's fast asleep!

PRINCE: *(doubtful)* Yes…but…that makes it worse, doesn't it? You can't just kiss a girl without asking. Not nowadays.

CINDERELLA: *(opening her eyes for a moment)* You *can* kiss me! I don't mind! *(She at once goes back to sleep)*

PRINCE: Oh well, that's all right then. *(He kisses her enthusiastically)* Wake up my sleeping beauty!

CINDERELLA: *(sleepily)* My darling Prince!

ROYAL SOOTHSAYER: Hippopotamus!

PRINCE: My gorgeous soon-to-be Princess!

ROYAL SOOTHSAYER: Hippopotamus!

CINDERELLA: But you didn't bring my shoe?

PRINCE: *(a touch annoyed)* No I didn't bring your shoe….

CINDERELLA: Never mind – you brought yourself – my sweet Prince

ROYAL SOOTHSAYER: Hippopotamus!

PRINCE: You lovely person!

ROYAL SOOTHSAYER: Hippopotamus!

PRINCE: *(losing it)* Will you *stop* saying Hippopotamus! This is the most romantic moment of my life and you're ruining it!

ROYAL SOOTHSAYER: I'm sorry my Liege! I can't help it! Do you think I *want* to say it?!

MUSIC

Song: The Hippopotamus Song

ROYAL SOOTHSAYER:
I feel such a silly clotamus, an awful idiotamus
Always finishing sentences by saying hippopotamus
It's such a silly word, and it's really quite absurd
I try hard not to say it, but I fear that I cannotamus....
Hippopotamus!

ALL JOIN IN FOR FOLLOWING VERSES:
Everywhere you go you hear an awful lot of rotamus
About the noble qualities this animal has gotamus.
He rolls around in mud, he's a thorough-going dud
An amazing smelly waste of space, a complete and absolute disgrace
Hippopotamus!

My favourite flower has always been the wild forgetmenotamus
My favourite living creature is the fearsome ocelotamus
But I couldn't give a fig, however small or big
For that ugly looking animal - I'd really like to ban 'em all
The Hippopotamus!

My favourite fruit, I'd like one now's, a juicy apricotamus
My favourite bird, lives by the sea's a lovely guillemotamus
But the creature I despise, it will come as no surprise
Is that good for nothing thimblerig, that dirty-looking jumped-up
pig... AAHHGH! Hippopotamus!

He feels such a silly clotamus, an awful idiotamus
Always finishing sentences by saying hippopotamus
It's the creature we despise, it will come as no surprise
Is that good-for-nothing thimblerig,
That dirty-looking jumped-up pig ...AAHHGH!
Hippopotamus!
Oh Yeah! *(They dance off)*

PRINCE: I'm sorry – you're quite right. It was mean of me to shout at you before. I'll have a word with Auntie Bertha and ask her to remove the spell when we get back to the palace.

ROYAL SOOTHSAYER: *(as in "thank you")* Hippopotamus.

PRINCE: And now my darling – all that remains for us to do is to get married and live happily ever after.

CINDERELLA: And get me a new shoe.

PRINCE: *(rather put out)* Yes, yes, of course – and get you a new shoe.

CINDERELLA: Now if you'll excuse me darling, I'm going to freshen up, in the hovel's bathroom.

PRINCE: Of course, my love.

CINDERELLA: *(going)* I can't wait to come back and live happily ever after!

PRINCE: Nor can I darling!

CINDERELLA: Bye bye!

PRINCE: Love you!

CINDERELLA: *(calling back)* Me too!

ROYAL SOOTHSAYER: My Liege, I don't want to put a damper on this happy occasion, but there is the small matter to consider of that unutterably evil goblin stealing your stepbrother, little Willie, from the Queen.

PRINCE: Oh my goodness, I'd quite forgotten that.

ROYAL SOOTHSAYER: Completely understandable my Liege. What with the excitement of all that kissing and stuff.

PRINCE: We must rush back home immediately and to stop him.

ROYAL SOOTHSAYER: I fear it's too late.

PRINCE: What do you mean?

ROYAL SOOTHSAYER: It will take hours to get back, and the goblin is due to collect the child in *(looks at his watch)* five minutes time.

PRINCE: Five minutes?!

ROYAL SOOTHSAYER: I'm afraid so, Your Royal Highness. We

can't help. It simply won't be possible.

They look at each other helplessly, and then turn to the audience

BOTH: Hippopotamus!

BLACKOUT & MUSIC

SCENE 6 – THE ROYAL DRAWING ROOM

Lights fade up on QUEEN (pacing up and down, with the baby in arms)

QUEEN: Oh woe is me! Any moment Melissa is going to come in and say "there's a goblin to see you" and my life will be ruined.

MELISSA: *(appearing)* There's a goblin to see you.

QUEEN: Not yet Melissa! Wait for your cue!

MELISSA: *(going)* Sorry, sorry.

KING: *(appearing from other side)* Hello my dear, Everything hunky-dory?

QUEEN: Don't be ridiculous Horace! It's anything *but* hunky-dory. 24 hours have gone by and we're still no nearer finding out the little beast's name.

KING: You told me it was Willy, didn't you

QUEEN: No, no – the goblin's name you idiot, not the baby's!

KING: Ah, yes of course. I'd forgotten all about that.

QUEEN: Soon I'll have to hand over the baby to him.

KING: Poor little Wally!

QUEEN: Little Willy!

KING: Little Willy!

QUEEN: I named him after you, you know.

Beat

KING: But my name's Horace

QUEEN: Horace William – *(meaningfully)* Willy for short.

KING: Ah gotcha. Yes.. Horace after my father, and William after…. Horace.

MELISSA: *(nervous, appearing)* Did you say "Hippopotamus Woof" My Lord?

KING: *(surprised)* Er…No. Should I have done?

MELISSA: It's my cue you see Sire.

KING: *(lost)* Right…

RUMPELSTILTSKIN

MELISSA: My cue to say "There's a goblin to see y-

QUEEN: *(interrupting)* Well he didn't say it Melissa. So go away and wait your turn.

MELISSA: *(mortified)* Yes, My Lady. *(exits)*

QUEEN: Honestly that girl Horace. If she wasn't your niece I would never have employed her.

KING: But she's not my niece. She told me she was *your* niece.

QUEEN: The little minx!

KING: Probably a bit confused I expect. It's often difficult to remember whose niece one is. I can never remember myself. Anyway – back to your goblin. Any idea of a name yet?

QUEEN: No idea at all.

KING: I was wondering about Gordon. Gordon Goblin – has a certain nobility about it don't you think?

QUEEN: No. It's a ridiculous name. Who in their right mind would call themselves Gordon?!

KING: There's Gordon the Big Engine.

QUEEN: Well he's not a goblin, is he?

KING: No. Good point. Was my brother any help? The Royal Soothsayer?

QUEEN: He was worse than useless. He had no idea of a name and spent most of our meeting saying "Hippopotamus Woof" *(pause while they wait for MELISSA to appear)*

QUEEN: I said – he spent most of our meeting saying *(shouts)* "Hippopotamus Woof"

MELISSA: *(rushes on to stage)* There's a Goblin to see you Sire!

QUEEN: About time Melissa!

MELISSA: Sorry my Lady.

KING: He didn't give you his name did he?

MELISSA: Yes

QUEEN/KING: What?!

MELISSA: He gave me his name when I answered the door.

QUEEN/KING: Well what is it!?

MELISSA: Er…. I've forgotten. I think it began with an "R"

KING: You've forgotten it!

QUEEN: Never mind. Never mind, let's get this over with.

KING: Show him in and take little Willy with you, Meriam.

QUEEN: Melissa!

KING: No, no – she said it began with an "R" – Melissa begins with an M.

MELISSA: *(off)* You can go in now goblin.

RUMPELSTILTSKIN: *(appearing)* Well hello Your Majesties. What a pleasure to see you both. And may I say Madam, for a woman who's just given birth, you look in splendid fettle.

QUEEN: Don't compliment me, you unutterably evil little goblin.

RUMPELSTILTSKIN: Now now, that's not what you said to me when I was spinning all that gold for you in the castle turret. You were nice as pie to me then.

QUEEN: Well I didn't have a firstborn son that you were going to cruelly snatch away from me.

RUMPELSTILTSKIN: But I've given you every chance to save him, haven't I? Three chances actually. You only have to guess my name.

KING: *(tentatively)* We were wondering about "Gordon Goblin"?

QUEEN: No we weren't…

RUMPELSTILTSKIN: Do you want to make that one of your guesses my Lord?

QUEEN: No we certainly don't!

KING: You're right my dear, it doesn't begin with R.

RUMPELSTILTSKIN: *(suspicious)* Who told you my name begins with "R".

KING: Nobody. Nobody – just a wild guess. And talking of wild guesses, how about….. Rudolph?

RUMPELSTILTSKIN: Wrong! One guess gone, two to go.

QUEEN: Er….might it be Rupert?

RUMPELSTILTSKIN: Rupert! Do I look like a Rupert?!! I'm a goblin, not a bear!

QUEEN: Sorry, sorry.

RUMPELSTILTSKIN: Nor a reindeer for that matter.

KING: Of course not. You haven't got a red nose.

RUMPELSTILTSKIN: You've got one guess left or the baby's mine. I'm off to use your loo – it will help build the dramatic suspense!

He leaves. The KING AND QUEEN look at each other helplessly.

QUEEN: *(sotto voce)* I've got an idea Horace.

KING: Yes?

QUEEN: We could ask the audience.

KING: Why would they know? Half of them are asleep…

QUEEN: It's our last chance. We've got to try something. Go on - ask them the question.

KING: *(to audience)* Oh very well. *(to audience)* Now audience – I've got a question for you. Do you believe in Fairies? If so clap your hands, and we can all save Tinkerbell -

QUEEN: No, no – not *that* question you fool!

KING: *(out of character)* Sorry…sorry….I was in *Peter Pan* last year, and I was getting confused.

QUEEN: Leave it to me Horace. *(to audience)* Tell me audience. Does anybody know the Goblin's name?

The audience shout Rumpelstiltskin's name

QUEEN: Rumpelstiltskin?

KING: That's a pretty rum name, Are you absolutely sure, audience?

AUDIENCE: YES!

KING: I think they're having us on dear….

QUEEN: Well I suppose we could try it. Nothing ventured, nothing gained.

KING: And it does begin with an R….

RUMPELSTILTSKIN: *(returning, doing up his flies)* Well? What's your third guess? I haven't got all day you know. I've got other unutterably evil things to do.

KING: Well…..we were thinking….

RUMPELSTILTSKIN: Yes?

QUEEN: Just a thought mind you.

RUMPELSTILTSKIN: Go on

KING: A bit of a wild guess really..

RUMPELSTILTSKIN: Get on with it!

QUEEN: Might it be…..

KING AND QUEEN: Rumpelstiltskin?

> *Beat*

RUMPELSTILTSKIN: WHO TOLD YOU!!!! WHO TOLD YOU!!! *(pointing at audience)* It was them wasn't it! I warned you all – I warned you I'd turn you all into jam doughnuts if you told them my name. Right. Here goes! You're jam doughnuts every one of you!

> *Fx spell sting*

RUMPELSTILTSKIN: Eh? What's happened? Why hasn't my spell worked? Why aren't you all doughnuts? It's that Witch, isn't it? She's put a restraining spell on me. It's not fair! IT'S NOT FAIR! *(He bursts into tears)*

> *Beat*

KING: I say old chap. Are you all right?

RUMPELSTILTSKIN: It's not fair! *(He sobs and collapses into the KING'S arms, sliding down his body as he speaks)* I never wanted to be unutterably evil. I just wanted to settle down in a happy marriage to my Sleeping Beauty, with a sweet baby like your little Willie.

KING: There there….

RUMPELSTILTSKIN: And now it's all been taken away from me! My whole life ruined! I've got no wife, no baby and no friends!

KING: Well you're talking to a man with a bit of experience of life, and I'd say that being unutterably evil is not necessarily the best way to attract friends.

RUMPELSTILTSKIN: Really?

KING: Be mildly offensive perhaps, but not unutterably evil.

RUMPELSTILTSKIN: I could give it a go, I suppose.

QUEEN: Do you have any interests - any hobbies? I always think that pursuing a hobby is a great way to meet people.

KING: That's why I took up golf.

RUMPELSTILTSKIN: Well I'm quite keen on gardening.

KING: Really? Well we've got a vacancy at the moment for an under-gardener in the Palace gardens. You could be just the man!

QUEEN: Or rather, just the goblin! *(They laugh. RUMPELSTILSKIN joins in just as they finish)*

KING: Meantime we could cheer ourselves up with a good song, couldn't we? One of my favourites is my twin brother's Hippopotamus song – do you know it? I'll play my brother – I'm rather good at it.

QUEEN: And the audience can all join in the Hippopotamuses!

KING: Excellent idea my dear! I'll just change my hat… (*as ROYAL SOOTHSAYER*) Right – off we go:

Song: The Hippopotamus Song (Reprise)

ROYAL SOOTHSAYER:
I feel such a silly clotamus, an awful idiotamus

Always finishing sentences by saying hippopotamus

It's such a silly word, and it's really quite absurd

I try hard not to say it, but I fear that I cannotamus….

Hippopotamus!

ALL JOIN IN FOR FOLLOWING VERSES:
Everywhere you go you hear an awful lot of rotamus

About the noble qualities this animal has gotamus.

He rolls around in mud, he's a thorough-going dud

An amazing smelly waste of space, a complete and absolute disgrace
Hippopotamus!

My favourite flower has always been the wild forgetmenotamus
My favourite living creature is the fearsome ocelotamus
But I couldn't give a fig, however small or big
For that ugly looking animal - I'd really like to ban 'em all
The Hippopotamus!

My favourite fruit, I'd like one now's, a juicy apricotamus
My favourite bird, lives by the sea's, a lovely guillemotamus
But the creature I despise, it will come as no surprise
Is that good for nothing thimblerig, that dirty-looking jumped-up pig…
AAHHGH! Hippopotamus!

He feels such a silly clotamus, an awful idiotamus
Always finishing sentences by saying hippopotamus
It's the creature we despise, it will come as no surprise
Is that good-for-nothing thimblerig,
That dirty-looking jumped-up pig
…AAHHGH!
Hippopotamus!
Oh Yeah!

ROYAL SOOTHSAYER: So little Willy grew up and became *big* Willy and was a credit to his mother and father.

QUEEN: And Cinderella married Prince Horace, who bought her a new pair of shoes every week, and they lived happily ever after.

RUMPELSTILTSKIN: And Rumpelstiltskin joined the Palace staff as a gardener, and there met a lovely girl called Melissa -

MELISSA: *(happy smile)* That's me!

RUMPELSTILTSKIN: - who became his wife. *(MELISSA and RUMPELSTILTSKIN look lovingly at each other while the cast go "ahhh!")*

MELISSA: And Rumpelstiltskin was put in charge of the King's vegetable patch where one day he grew a beanstalk so large that it stretched all the way up into the sky and his young apprentice, an elf called Jack, climbed up it and -

ROYAL SOOTHSAYER: *(interrupting)* But that's another story. It's time to go home now. But as you do so, I want you all to remember that even the most unutterably evil goblin can be redeemed by a kind word, a steady job and the love of a good woman. *(beat)* Or a man. *(beat)* Or anyone on the gender spectrum.

Rumpelstiltskin holds up panel that says "MORAL OF PLAY"

Yes – that's the moral of our play.

ALL: Hippopotamus!

CURTAIN

SNOW WHITE AND THE BIG BAD WOLF

First performance at Colour House Theatre, Easter 2022

ORIGINAL CAST:
KING HORACE/ROYAL SOOTHSAYER: Neil Summerville
MELISSA/SNOW WHITE: Lucy Sprekley
JOLLY/WOLF: Sam Peterson
MORGANA/WITCH: Maria McGurl
MIRROR (RECORDED VOICE): Alan Bennett

SCENES

SCENE 1 - The Royal Throne Room
SCENE 2 - The Royal Drawing Room
SCENE 3 - The Wild Wood
SCENE 4 - The Royal Drawing Room
SCENE 5 - The Wild Wood
SCENE 6 - The Royal Drawing Room
SCENE 7 - A Cottage in the Wild Wood
SCENE 8 - The Royal Drawing Room

SCENE 1 – THE ROYAL THRONE ROOM

The curtain opens to reveal KING HORACE, crown askew and legs dangling over an easy chair, munching his way through a rapidly diminishing pile of muffins. His face is streaked with butter and his shirt sleeves covered in jam. He seems surprised but unconcerned to find himself the centre of attention

KING: *(noticing the audience)* Ah – hello. Just having a muffin. You can't beat them. Some people prefer toasted teacakes of course – or hot buttered scones dripping with honey - but I've always been a muffin-man myself.

Fancy one little girl? You do? Well sorry about that. I'm afraid there are none left! *(and indeed there aren't; the King has just shoved the last one into his mouth.)* Another time perhaps…

Never mind - look I'll sing you a song about muffins if you like….would you like that? You would?

MELISSA: *(entering)* There's a dwarf to see you Sire…

KING: What?

MELISSA: There's a dwarf to see -

KING: *(angry)* Oh no there isn't

MELISSA: Oh yes there is…

KING: Oh no there *isn't!* Not yet! I haven't sung my muffin song yet. Your cue is "Ed Sheeran eat your heart out……"

MELISSA: *(thinks)* You're right Sire! That's amazing! How did you know that?

KING: Because we've been rehearsing it for the last two weeks….

MELISSA: So we have! Yes. You sing a song now, don't you?

KING: *(gritted teeth)* Yes!

MELISSA: You sing it awfully well Sire.

KING: *(mollified a little)* Really? You think so?

MELISSA: Yes. For an old man you're really not bad.

KING: *(gritted teeth)* Thank you Meriam.

MELISSA: Melissa Sire. Meriam is the Royal Schoolmistress.

KING: Ah yes. Taught me everything I know. Which isn't much.

MELISSA: And I'm First Lady of the Queen's Bedchamber.

KING: Gotcha

MELISSA: Though with the Queen visiting her sick mother in Weybridge, there's not much for me to do Sire.

KING: *(uninterested)* Really?

MELISSA: Apart from announce the arrival of dwarves and stuff….

KING: Look I've got a song to sing….Could you possibly -

MELISSA: You must miss her dreadfully Sire.

KING: Miss who?

MELISSA: The Queen.

KING: Ah yes. The Queen! Yes. Of course I do…. Dreadfully……Dreadfully … Now would you please mind –

MELISSA: Though Morgana must be a great comfort to you.

KING: Morgana?

MELISSA: The Queen's cousin Sire. Who's here to "keep an eye on you." That's what the Queen told me.

KING: Dreadful woman.

MELISSA: The Queen?

KING: No, no – the Morgan woman. Vain as a peacock. Struts around the palace mouthing off at mirrors.

MELISSA: I like her niece, Snow White. She's a really nice girl. She told me that-

KING: Look Matilda, these good people here are waiting for me to sing a song. So would you please just get off the stage and let me sing it.

MELISSA: *(rather hurt)* Very well Sire. I was only trying to be friendly….. *(She reluctantly leaves)*

KING: Yes. Right. Where was I? I was going to sing you a song, wasn't I? *(to audience)* Any idea what about?

Audience hopefully say 'muffins'

MELISSA: *(sticks head through curtain)* You can't beat a muffin!

KING: What at? Ah no….That's my song, isn't it. Yes, yes. Thank you

Mildred! *(calls out to unseen sound operator)* Music Thingy!

Song: (KING AND CHORUS) "You Can't Beat a Muffin"

KING:
(under intro) Oh Yeah!
Oh there's nuffin like a muffin when you're feeling like a snack
Smother it in butter, and there'll be no looking back
Stuff it in your mouth, or lingeringly lick it
Just make sure that no one comes along and tries to nick it

The other cast members dance on to join the KING sing the next two lines

CHORUS AND KING:
You can't beat a muffin
There's absolutely nuffin

KING:
There's nuffin like a muffin every day.

CHORUS:
You can't beat a muffin
There's absolutely nuffin

KING:
I wouldn't have it any other way.

The CHORUS dances as the KING prepares for his second verse

KING:
Now there's folk out there who'd rather have a scone,
A cake or a biscuit - but I think they might be wrong
Add honey on the butter - make sure it's piping hot
A muffin, when it's toasted, is more scrumptious than the lot

CHORUS AND KING:
You can't beat a muffin
There's absolutely nuffin

KING:
There's nuffin like a muffin when it's hot.

CHORUS AND KING:
No you can't beat a muffin
There's absolutely nuffin

KING:
Should anyone deny, they're talking rot!

More exuberant dancing from the chorus

KING:
Oh yeah!

CHORUS:
Oh yeah!

KING:
My brother likes bananas, but they fill me with revulsion
And eating prunes or apples always gives me a convulsion
Brussels sprouts and cauliflowers just bring me out in spots
I'd advise you all to throw out every vegetable you've got

CHORUS AND KING:
You can't beat a muffin
There's absolutely nuffin

KING:
There's nuffin like a muffin every day.

CHORUS AND KING:
No you can't beat a muffin
There's absolutely nuffin

KING:
There's nuffin like a muffin every day.
One more time!

CHORUS AND KING:
You can't beat a muffin
There's absolutely nuffin

KING:
There's nuffin like a muffin every day.

The CHORUS dance off – but as they leave they turn back to the audience and as the music ends say

CHORUS:
There's absolutely nuffin!

KING: Wasn't that brilliant? Ed Sheeran eat your heart out!

MELISSA: *(enters)* There's a dwarf to see you Sire!

KING: Seven dwarves surely?

MELISSA: No – just the one Sire. I've shown him into the Royal Drawing Room

KING: That's odd. The Royal Soothsayer definitely said there would be seven of 'em, Melinda.

MELISSA: Melissa

KING: That's what I said wasn't it? *(turns to audience for confirmation)* Wasn't it?

AUDIENCE: No

KING: No matter! This dwarf is going to be the saviour of the Kingdom! It's been prophesied. Lead me to him! *(calls off)* Dim the lights Thingy! *(blackout)* I said *dim* them you idiot. Not a complete blackout! *(trips over set)* I've got to change the furniture! Ow! I can't see a thing. What's this squishy stuff?.

MELISSA: It's me Sire.

KING: Get out the way you silly woman. Music! Music! Play some music!

Some music is played

SCENE 2 – THE ROYAL DRAWING ROOM

JOLLY is seated waiting for the KING, who enters a little discombobulated...

JOLLY: (*bowing*) Your Royal Highness.

KING: (*surprised*) Ah hello Thingy. I'm looking for a dwarf.

JOLLY: Good morning my Liege. I'm Jolly.

KING: Good, good. Glad to hear it. Load of moaning minnies round here… I'm always happy to meet a jolly chappie.

JOLLY: No, no – That's my name. I'm Jolly the Dwarf.

KING: Really? *(looks carefully at him)* You're tall for a dwarf.

JOLLY: We prefer to be called "persons of short stature" Sire.

KING: OK – well you're tall for a person of short stature.

JOLLY: (*uncomfortable*) You could say that Sire.

KING: I did say that Sire. And where are the other six of you? The prophecy was for seven dwarves. I've got a job for you all.

JOLLY: Er….they're waiting in the wings.

KING: Good, good. Show 'em in. I've got their names somewhere…. *(pulls out paper)* The Royal Schoolmistress wrote them out for me, Yes…here we are…. Doc, Bashful, Sneez……

JOLLY: (*quickly*) No no – Disney have the copyright on those names

KING: Ah yes …well, what are your chaps called Jilly?

JOLLY: Jolly

KING: What – all seven of 'em? Bit unimaginative that.

JOLLY: No no Sire –

KING: And difficult to know who's who eh? *Jolly* difficult *(Laughs at his own joke)*

JOLLY: No Jolly's me Sire. Er….. I'll just go and get the others.

KING: Jolly good. Get a move on then.

JOLLY then runs from stage left to stage right acting each dwarf in turn, in increasingly frenetic fashion

JOLLY: I'm Sniffly My Liege *(blows his nose)*

KING: Wipe your nose

JOLLY: I'm Clumsy *(tripping over his feet)*

KING: You certainly are…

JOLLY: I'm Scary *(attempts to scare KING)*

KING: Good Lord! Have a care will you?

JOLLY: And I'm Smelly

KING: Yuk…. *(holds nose in disgust)* You're disgusting.

JOLLY: I'm Hammy

KING: You're in the right production then… (*laughs*)

JOLLY: And I'm Jeremy

KING: Wait a sec! Jeremy! You look familiar…

JOLLY: (*exhausted*] And I'm Jolly….tired….*(He collapses in front of KING, for whom the penny is just beginning to drop.)*

KING: Hold on…hold on….there's something rum about this. You say you're Jolly. But you were Jeremy as well, weren't you. Wasn't he? *(He turns to audience for confirmation. Hopefully someone will shout "he was all of them")*

KING: *(in response to audience)* He was *all* of 'em?

JOLLY: OK! OK! I admit it my Liege. I *was* Scary. And I was Sniffly, and Clumsy and Smelly and Hammy and Jeremy as well.

KING: My goodness. You could have fooled me.

JOLLY: I think I *did* fool you My Liege

KING: So why aren't there seven of you as I requested?

JOLLY: Er…There are two reasons for that Sire…..

KING: Which are?

JOLLY: Well firstly…..I outgrew the other six.

KING: You what?

JOLLY: I got bigger and bigger until I couldn't fit into my bed Sire. Or the room. Or the cottage for that matter. I couldn't stop growing! I had to leave the other six dwarves and make my own way in the world.

KING: Good Lord! And what was the other reason?

JOLLY: The producer couldn't afford seven dwarves Sire. He's tight as a drum.

KING: *(out of character)* Don't I know it! Do you know what I'm getting paid for this gig?

Beat

JOLLY: *(out of character)* You're getting *paid* for it?

Uncomfortable pause

KING: Anyway. Anyway. The fact is Jilly –

JOLLY: Jolly! *(who thinking about the previous speech is certainly not jolly!)*

KING: The fact is Jolly, things aren't terribly perky on the money front just at the moment. So I'm in urgent need of a dwarf to find the thousand gold coins that my Great Uncle Horatio buried in the heart of the Wild Wood forty seven years ago, to prevent them being stolen by Frost Giants.

JOLLY: But there's no such thing as Frost Giants.

KING: Yes…but Great Uncle Horatio thought there were. He was going a bit doolally. It runs in the family.

JOLLY: Where exactly is the money buried My Liege?

KING: Well that's the point. I don't know, do I! If I did I wouldn't be asking you to find it for me.

JOLLY: But why ask *me*?

KING: Because it's been prophesied! By my twin brother the Royal Soothsayer. He can look into the future. He knows things.

JOLLY: What's he prophesied?

KING: That one of the seven dwarves who live in the cottage in the forest would find the money for us and save the Kingdom from penury.

JOLLY: Penury?

KING: Stop us getting broke. Keep us in muffins – that sort of thing.

JOLLY: Well now I no longer live in the cottage in the forest, that rather disqualifies me doesn't it?

KING: I don't see why. After all you *used* to live there. Before you had your growing spurt.

JOLLY: (*doubtful*) I suppose so….

KING: And there'll be a big reward for you if you find the money. *When* you find the money.

JOLLY: (*jolly*) A big reward?

They are interrupted by the arrival of MORGANA and SNOW WHITE

MORGANA: (*appearing*) Ah Horace – there you are! I've been looking for you everywhere.

KING: Really? You should have tried here.

MORGANA: (*unimpressed by Jolly*) And who's this little man? He looks like an overgrown dwarf.

KING: Bullseye! That's exactly what he is. Jilly, Jolly, Polly – this is my wife's cousin – er…

MORGANA: Morgana

KING: More what?

MORGANA: Gana!

KING: She's called Gana. And this is her niece – Snow Black.

MORGANA: Snow White!

KING: Snow What….

SNOW WHITE: (*looking lovingly at JOLLY*) We know each other Auntie. We've met in the forest. Several times.

MORGANA: (*disdainfully*) Have you now?

JOLLY: (*enthusiastically*) It was really jolly…

MORGANA: Well don't you be getting ideas above your station young man. My niece is not for the likes of you.

KING: I say – that's a bit harsh isn't it? Jilly is going to find me a thousand gold coins, and when he does I'm going to give him one all for himself.

JOLLY: (*disappointed*) One?

MORGANA: Your generosity knows no bounds Horace.

KING: Yes, yes...now look if you'll excuse me Margarita –

MORGANA: Morgana!

KING: *(looks round)* Where?

MORGANA: Here!

KING: Ah yes. Hello....Anyway, I've got to take this young fella to meet my brother the Royal Soothsayer and begin the hunt for the treasure.

MORGANA: But I wanted to talk to you Horace about the appalling state of the Royal Beauty Parlour

KING: Yes...well...some other time perhaps. Molly – hop to it! You've got work to do! *(He goes)*

SNOW WHITE: Goodbye my friend. Be jolly! I'll see you soon.

MORGANA: You most certainly will not. I forbid you to leave the palace without my permission.

SNOW WHITE: (*appalled*) But Auntie!

MORGANA: Now go and get me my handbag which I've left in my bedroom,

SNOW WHITE: (*dolefully*) Yes Auntie.

Everyone goes leaving MORGANA alone.

MORGANA: Good. That's got rid of her. Now then *(She surveys the audience)* Wow you're an ugly audience aren't you? But then few people are as beautiful as me. Tell me child, do you think I am the most beautiful woman in the world?

CHILD: "No"

MORGANA: What a ridiculous response. You need to go to Specsavers. Let me ask someone with a bit more experience of life . This mirror for instance. *(confidentially to a child)* This is a mirror-call...

Mirror, mirror, on the wall, who's the fairest of them all?

MIRROR: *(recorded voice)* You mean in this room – or in the whole world?

MORGANA: Well obviously I mean in the whole world, you thick piece of glass

MIRROR: Well....it's not you!

MORGANA: *What*?!!

MIRROR: There's a very nice young lady in Kolkata who people say is one of the -

MORGANA: Never mind ladies in Kolkata! Let's start again shall we? Who's the fairest of them all in this room.

MIRROR: You are.

MORGANA: Good. Right – now who's the fairest of them all in the palace?

MIRROR: Hold on a sec. I'm taking that back. You're not the fairest of them all in this room anymore.

MORGANA: What do you mean? Who on earth is?

MIRROR: She's behind you!

MORGANA turns around in horror to see, in a spotlight SNOW WHITE, who has reappeared with MORGANA'S handbag

MORGANA: Snow White! (*beat*) Where's my apple....?

A sinister music sting and blackout. Music.

SCENE 3 – THE WILD WOOD

The ROYAL SOOTHSAYER and JOLLY are following a woodland path

ROYAL SOOTHSAYER: This way young man! Get a move on!

JOLLY: I'm coming My Lord. It's just that I'm not feeling very jolly

ROYAL SOOTHSAYER: But you *are* Jolly.

JOLLY: I'm miserable if you must know. Kicked out of my own home. No friends in the world. And now I'm in love with a woman I'll never be allowed to marry.

ROYAL SOOTHSAYER: Really?

JOLLY: Really. Let me explain:

Song: It's Awful Being Jolly

JOLLY:
It's awful being Jolly when I really feel quite mad
And though others may say "golly – things can't really be that bad!"
I assure you I'm not lying
For I often feel like crying.
Just be happy you're not Jolly, or you'll end up jolly sad

CHORUS:
Just be happy you're not Jolly, or you'll end up jolly sad

JOLLY:
I was once a happy chappie, a young dwarf, just one of seven
We had a cottage in the country – it was blissful, down in Devon
But then I began to grow
The others said I had to go
They kicked me out, and so I had to leave my little taste of heaven

CHORUS:
They kicked him out, and so he had to leave his little taste of heaven

JOLLY:
To add salt into the wound, and this surely isn't right
I've met a woman whom I love, she is my joy and my delight
Yet her mean and wicked aunt

SNOW WHITE

> Says forget her – but I can't
> I shall worship her forever, for there'll never be another Snow White
> **CHORUS:**
> Yes he'll worship her forever, for there'll never be another Snow White
> **CHORUS AND JOLLY:**
> He/I will worship her forever for there'll never be another Snow White

ROYAL SOOTHSAYER: Cheer up my boy. You never know what's round the corner.

JOLLY: Well, you'd know, wouldn't you?

ROYAL SOOTHSAYER: What?

JOLLY: Being the Royal Soothsayer, you know everything.

ROYAL SOOTHSAYER: *(doubtful)* Er…yes…….. well I confidently predict that round the corner is… another tree.

JOLLY: Never mind trees! Will I ever marry Snow White? If not I don't think I'll be able to bear it.

ROYAL SOOTHSAYER: Woof.

JOLLY: Pardon

ROYAL SOOTHSAYER: Hippopotamus Woof!

JOLLY: Are you all right?

ROYAL SOOTHSAYER: Sorry. Sorry. I've been cursed by the Queen's sister – the Witch. Any mention of an animal and I'm forced to bark.

JOLLY: So when I said I couldn't *bear* it…

ROYAL SOOTHSAYER: Woof!

JOLLY: I see what you mean. And what about the Hippopotamus bit?

ROYAL SOOTHSAYER: Woof.

JOLLY: Sorry, sorry – shouldn't have said Hippopotamus.

ROYAL SOOTHSAYER: Woof. No, you see what makes it worse is that whenever anyone says a word beginning with the letter "P"

– Hippopotamus Woof - I'm forced to say "Hippopotamus". Woof.

JOLLY: But why do you Woof as well as saying Hippopotamus?

ROYAL SOOTHSAYER: Woof. Because it's an animal, isn't it?

PRINCE: Hippopotamus?

ROYAL SOOTHSAYER: Woof. Precisely. Hippopotamus. Woof.

JOLLY: Wow. And I thought *I* had problems

ROYAL SOOTHSAYER: Hippopotamus Woof! That witch. *(spits out the name)* Bertha. I loathe her! I'd like to march up behind her and stick her broomstick right up her –

A bang - smoke - and the WITCH appears.

WITCH: Right up my what Tiresias?

ROYAL SOOTHSAYER: Oh Heavens – it's you!

WITCH: You have an extraordinary capacity for stating the obvious, don't you…Precious.

ROYAL SOOTHSAYER: Hippopotamus Woof!

WITCH: It's really… pitiful.

ROYAL SOOTHSAYER: Hippopotamus Woof!

WITCH: If totally predictable

ROYAL SOOTHSAYER: Hippopotamus Woof.

WITCH: You know I really think we can improve on his curse. *(She waves her wand and there's a bang)*

JOLLY: What have you done?

WITCH: From now on every time he barks, he will also bleat…like a lamb

ROYAL SOOTHSAYER: Woof Baa….

WITCH: Like that. Perfect!

ROYAL SOOTHSAYER: *(angrily)* Hippopotamus Woof Baa!

WITCH: It's so enjoyable being a witch Jolly! You should try it sometime. You can have such fun!

JOLLY: How did you know my name?

WITCH: I'm a witch. I know everybody's names. I know that in the audience today there's a *(says names of two selected audience members and finishes with the name Peter)*

ROYAL SOOTHSAYER: Hippopotamus Woof Baa

WITCH: Now if you'll excuse me I must be off. I'm on the trail of a big bad wolf. See you again soon I hope Tiresias – Probably! *(She goes off, laughing)*

ROYAL SOOTHSAYER: *(angrily back at her)* Hippopotamus Woof Baa!

JOLLY: A big bad wolf!

ROYAL SOOTHSAYER: Woof Baa!

JOLLY: Oh my goodness Tiresias, I do hope my Snow White won't come to any harm.

ROYAL SOOTHSAYER: I wouldn't know about that.

JOLLY: I thought you knew everything?

ROYAL SOOTHSAYER: There some things, Jolly, that are hidden even from me.

JOLLY: What a pity!

ROYAL SOOTHSAYER: Hippopotamus Woof Baa!

MELISSA: *(making an unscheduled entrance)* All is well. Snow White has been rescued and the thousand gold coins have been found!

JOLLY AND ROYAL SOOTHSAYER: What!!

MELISSA: All is well. Snow White has been rescued and –

ROYAL SOOTHSAYER: Melissa! We're not even halfway through yet. What are you burbling on about?

MELISSA: But that was my cue – Hippopotamus, Woof, Baa.

ROYAL SOOTHSAYER: Woof Baa.

JOLLY: Melissa dear – you say that speech in the final scene – not now.

MELISSA: Sorry. Sorry. Should I have said "There's a dwarf to see you Sire"? That's one of my other speeches.

ROYAL SOOTHSAYER: No you shouldn't!

MELISSA: Or there's "I just know that's she run away from the evil Piers Morgan. "

ROYAL SOOTHSAYER: Hippopotamus Woof! It's the evil Morgana!" - Just get off the stage woman!

MELISSA: All right. All right! I was just trying to do my job *(she leaves, tail between legs)*

ROYAL SOOTHSAYER: Honestly! I despair! How long have we had to rehearse this?!

JOLLY: She's doing her best,

ROYAL SOOTHSAYER: Well it's not good enough. Anyway. We have a job to do. To find those a thousand golden coins.

JOLLY: Right you are Tiresias. Follow me. This looks a likely path

ROYAL SOOTHSAYER: *(energetically)* Hippopotamus Woof Baa!

BLACKOUT AND MUSIC

SCENE 4 – THE ROYAL DRAWING ROOM

MORGANA is addressing the mirror.

MORGANA: Right Mirror. Let's try again shall we. I'm giving you one more chance.

MIRROR: Off you go then…

MORGANA: Mirror, mirror on the wall, who's the fairest of them all……in this room

MIRROR: You are.

MORGANA: Good, good – that's more like it. Now then – Mirror, mirror on the wall, who's the fairest of them all, in this palace?

MIRROR: You are.

MORGANA: Excellent. Now then - Mirror, mirror on the –

MIRROR: Look, just skip the rhyme will you – you're boring me.

MORGANA: OK. OK. Who's the fairest of them all in this Kingdom?

MIRROR: Snow White

MORGANA: What! Who did you say?!!! How dare you!

MIRROR: If you don't want a truthful answer don't ask the question.

MORGANA: You said I was the fairest of them all *in this palace*.

MIRROR: That's because Snow White is in the woods looking for her boyfriend.

MORGANA: How dare she! I expressly forbad her to see that jumped-up dwarf!

MIRROR: Why should she take any notice of you?

MORGANA: How dare you speak to me like that ! *(She turns to audience and picks on a child)* I'm the most beautiful woman in the whole wide world, whatever that stupid mirror says. *(turns to another audience member)* Tell me, who do you think is more beautiful – me, or Snow White? *(reacts accordingly)* Well we'll settle the question once and for all. *(She brings out a shiny apple from her pocket and offers it to the first child she spoke to)* Would you like a nice juicy apple darling? No – I should think not. Because I've poisoned it! One bite of this and you'll never have to go to school again! Would you like that?

Now my silly niece is always going on about how an apple a day keeps the doctor away. Well we'll see about that. I'm going to leave this apple here – and you can bet anything you like that Snow White will eat it. And then I won't care at all if people find her more beautiful than me – because she'll be *dead*!!! And dead people don't count!

Laughs as she exits the room. There's a pause and then KING HORACE comes in from one entrance and SNOW WHITE from another

KING: I say. Who are you? You can't just come wandering in here without -

SNOW WHITE: I've just been out for a walk my Liege. I'm Snow White.

KING: Course you are. Course you are Snowy. I was just testing you. You're the niece of Queen Whatsername, aren't you?

SNOW WHITE: Queen Whatshername?

KING: That's the one. I should know. I married her! Can't think why….

SNOW WHITE: Well I'm sure she's –

KING: Oh yes – she's better than that awful Morgan woman. Do you know her?

SNOW WHITE: She's my Aunt Sire.

KING: *(sympathetically)* Course she is. Poor you!

SNOW WHITE: I was wondering Sire if –

KING: Lunch? You want your lunch? Absolutely. I'm starving – I could eat a horse!

SNOW WHITE: I'm not really very hungry Sire.

KING: Never mind. All the more for me eh?

SNOW WHITE: Yes Sire

KING: Right – I'm off to the Royal Stables! Toodlepip! *(He leaves)*

SNOW WHITE: *(sighs sadly – then notices audience)* Oh - Hello everyone. It's so nice to see you. I need cheering up. What are your names? – shout them out to me. *(the audience does: she picks on one of them)* …….. – That's a lovely name. I had a rabbit called .... He was eaten by a fox.

You know, I'm feeling rather lonely here in this big palace. Can I sing you a song about it? *(to Sound Technician)* Play the music please.

Snow White's Song – What Should I Do?

SNOW WHITE:
I know that I'm lucky –
I don't want your pity
Life's not always easy
It's hard and it's gritty
My mother has died
And I live with my aunt
I wish that I loved her
I've tried - but I can't

CHORUS:
She's tried….. but she can't

SNOW WHITE:
I've tried…… but I can't
She says she's a beauty
I'm sure that that's true
She has many admirers
She tells me - Me too!
But her beauty is skin deep
It's not in her soul
That's where real beauty lies
That's what makes people whole

CHORUS:
That's what makes people whole

SNOW WHITE:
That's what makes people whole.
My Jolly's not handsome
But he's loving and kind
He's got a beautiful soul
And a beautiful mind
And that's what's important

Gives purpose to life
We want to get married
Be husband and wife

CHORUS:
Be husband and wife

SNOW WHITE:
Be husband and wife
But my aunt can't abide him
She's horrid and mean
She's vain as a peacock
And wants to be Queen
She forbids me to see him
She's brimming with malice
She keeps me a prisoner
Trapped here in the palace

CHORUS:
Trapped here.... in the palace

SNOW WHITE:
Trapped here...... in the palace
Oh what can I do – oh where should I go?

CHORUS:
We'd all love to help you – Alas, we don't know.
Don't know. Don't know. Don't know.

SNOW WHITE: Well – there's no point being sad. I shall cheer myself up by eating this apple. After all, an apple a day keeps the doctor away! *(She walks towards the apple and picks it up – hopefully the audience will start shouting for her not to eat it. If they don't she asks them for advice – so this bit ad-libbed accordingly....)* Do you think I should eat one of the King's apples without asking his permission. No? Why not? It's *poisoned*!!! Who on earth would have poisoned it? MY *aunt*!!! She'd never do a thing like that.... Oh no she wouldn't (*etc*) Really? My Auntie Morgana wants to kill me? Why? Because I'm more beautiful than her? That's *awful*. I shall have to escape to the Wild Wood before she finds me. Oh dear – I wish my lovely Jolly was here to help me. What am I going to do? What

am I going to do?
BLACKOUT AND MUSIC

SCENE 5 – THE WILD WOOD

The WITCH enters to the usual accompaniment of smoke and thunder. She addresses the audience directly.

WITCH: Oh – you're still here are you. If you had any sense you'd have walked out by now – I would have done. Still the good news is that you can hear me sing my Witch's song. Would you like that? It's the same as in last year's play, but so what! We can't keep composing new songs for you – we're not made of money. Anyway, the writer spends most of his time on Wimbledon Common Golf course nowadays; he last had an original thought ten years ago. So – music please ……….. Now!

Witch's Song

WITCH:
You don't get rich,
Being a Witch….
But it's fun.
You don't get rich
Being a Witch.
For if I give my wand a twirl
I can turn you little girl
Into a scrumptious currant bun.
O yes I could – perhaps I should
Get on my broom,
Fly round this room
And make a chicken casserole of
Everyone….

But don't despair.
I'm very fair
Ask anyone.
But don't despair.
I'm very fair.
If you treat me with respect,
Admire my fearsome intellect,

SNOW WHITE

Then we'll have fun.
In retrospect
We'll have a ball.
But if you make me hopping mad
I can be very, very bad
Turn your fingers into butter,
Throw your toys into the gutter,
Every one...

Every Witch
Must have a cat
I can't stand mine.
For every Witch must have a cat
My cat is called Matilda
Several times I've nearly killed her
But then again, a cat has got nine lives.
She is lazy and pernicious
And occasionally vicious
A crazy mixed-up mog
Who thinks she is a dog
Can you believe it?

But I'm so glad
That I'm so bad
It's a laugh.
Yes, I'm so glad
That I'm bad.
I gave myself three wishes
Never wash or dry the dishes
I never floss between my teeth
Nor have a bath.
My bedroom's a disgrace
Looks like someone's trashed the place,
But nothing goes to waste
Cos my magic spells are ace!

Yes, I'm a witch! A lovely witch!
Yes, I'm a witch! I'm a witch, I'm a wi…..tch. I'm a WITCH!

WITCH: There. That was so much better than wimpy Snow White's song eh? *(addresses a girl in the audience)* Wasn't that the most brilliant display of singing you ever heard? Don't you give me any cheek young lady or for the rest of your life I'll have you saying "Hippopotamus, Woof, Baa"

MELISSA: *(enter ROYAL SOOTHSAYER)* All is well. Snow White has been rescued and the thousand gold coins have been found!

WITCH: Wrong scene Melissa! Buzz off!

MELISSA: Sorry….. *(She exits quickly)*

WITCH: *(back to the child she has picked on)* Stupid woman! Now – where was I? Would you like to say Hippopotamus, Woof Baa, for the rest of your life? No? Let's have a practice shall we. Up on the stage, Come on. Now when I wave my wand say Hippopotamus Woof Baa. *(child does this)* Come on – put some feeling into it. It's a huge Hippopotamus, an angry dog, and a loud bleating lamb. *(She demonstrates)* Hippopotamus. Woof. Baa. Right try again. *(comments appropriately on child's attempt)*

We'll let you know dear. Now sit down – I can't hang around talking to the likes of you. I've got a big bad wolf to find. *(the wolf's head - worn by actor playing Snow White - appears behind her)* Anybody seen him, *(shouts from audience – ad lib from WITCH as she pointedly looks in the wrong direction each time)* Where? There? Don't be ridiculous. There? Stop wasting my time. You're extremely lucky I haven't turned you all into tuna fish sandwiches. Next time I will, I promise you! *(She goes)*

Meantime from the theatre foyer come the ROYAL SOOTHSAYER & JOLLY – the ROYAL SOOTHSAYER is carrying a metal detector which he uses at appropriate times

ROYAL SOOTHSAYER: Right – this way Jolly. I have a good feeling about this way. It's my Scottish upbringing you know – We learn to smell where the money is! Right – let's start detectoring eh? *(puts on headphones and starts – conversation carries on through this)*

JOLLY: It's my turn to be detectorer!

ROYAL SOOTHSAYER: No it isn't. It's mine. *(pause for some detectoring)*

JOLLY: Why were you educated in Scotland?

ROYAL SOOTHSAYER: To keep me away from my twin brother the King. Nobody could tell us apart, so they sent me to live with my Auntie Jean in Glasgow.

JOLLY: That explains the dodgy Scottish accent

ROYAL SOOTHSAYER: Exactly. What do you mean dodgy?

JOLLY: Nothing, nothing.

(Silence while they detect some more)

ROYAL SOOTHSAYER: Not a flicker on this thing. We've been searching for hours, and we've found nothing.

JOLLY: I wonder where my Snow White is? I miss her so much. Do you know her awful aunt won't let her see me again? The rotten cow!

ROYAL SOOTHSAYER: Woof Baa

JOLLY: Sorry, sorry – I forgot I mustn't mention any animals.

ROYAL SOOTHSAYER: Or words beginning with…you know… that letter…..

JOLLY: What letter?

ROYAL SOOTHSAYER: The one after 'O'.

JOLLY: Er…. P!

ROYAL SOOTHSAYER: Hippopotamus Woof Baa.

MELISSA: *(enters quickly)* All is well. Snow White has been rescued and the thousand gold coins have been found!

ROYAL SOOTHSAYER: *Not yet* Melissa!

MELISSA: But that's my cue. It must be the final scene by now. It's been going on for ages!

ROYAL SOOTHSAYER: It only *seems* ages.

JOLLY: Melissa will you go – please!

ROYAL SOOTHSAYER: Hippopotamus Woof Baa

MELISSA: All is well. Snow White has been rescued and –

ROYAL SOOTHSAYER: No no!

JOLLY: For pity's sake -

ROYAL SOOTHSAYER: Hippopotamus Woof Baa -

MELISSA: All is well. Snow White has been -

ROYAL SOOTHSAYER: Will you stop burbling on about Snow White being rescued!

JOLLY: *(worried at this thought)* Well we should, perhaps,-

ROYAL SOOTHSAYER: Hippopotamus Woof Baa -

MELISSA: All is well. Snow White has been rescued -

JOLLY: We should possibly -

ROYAL SOOTHSAYER: Hippopotamus Woof Baa -

MELISSA: All is well. Snow White -

JOLLY: Please!

ROYAL SOOTHSAYER: Hippopotamus Woof Baa -

MELISSA: All is well. Snow White has been rescued and -–

ROYAL SOOTHSAYER: *(losing it completely)* If you don't shut up about Snow White I am going to go stark, staring bonkers!!!

(Beat)

MELISSA: *(hurt)* Sorry! Sorry! There's no need for that sort of language.

ROYAL SOOTHSAYER: *(a little ashamed)* I apologise. I don't know what came over me.

MELISSA: I forgive you. And just to cheer you up here's a gold coin for both of you. *(She produces two from her apron)*

JOLLY: What?

ROYAL SOOTHSAYER: Where did you get those?

MELISSA: I found them in the forest. I was walking through the woods looking for you so that I could say my line "All is well. Snow White has been rescued –

ROYAL SOOTHSAYER: Yes, yes, never mind that. Where did you

find this gold?

MELISSA: Well I tripped over a tree stump – and guess what – it was hollow, and full of – I'd say – at least a thousand gold coins! I'm going to be rich!

ROYAL SOOTHSAYER: No you're not. That money belongs to the King! *(afterthought)* And his twin brother.

MELISSA: Who's that?

ROYAL SOOTHSAYER: Well me obviously!

MELISSA: Of course! I remember now. That's why you look so like him.

ROYAL SOOTHSAYER: *(a new thought)* But Melissa…..if you were to.. er.. not tell him who actually *found* the gold, so that he thinks it was Jolly and myself, then I'd make sure you were amply rewarded. Say three gold coins and no questions asked?

MELISSA: What – you mean three gold coins instead of the thousand gold coins I've already got?

ROYAL SOOTHSAYER: Er…yes…

MELISSA: *(thinks about it, then cheerfully)* OK. That sounds fair to me.

JOLLY: But Melissa…..you say in your speech that you haven't said yet, that Snow White had been rescued….. Rescued from what?

MELISSA: I've no idea. (*this said in one breath*) I just know that she's run away from her evil Auntie Morgana who was trying to kill her, and is now wandering through the deep wild wood, cold, hungry and homeless, hoping to be jolly.

ROYAL: SOOTHSAYER *(as actor giving her a prompt)* Hoping to *find* Jolly.

MELISSA: Sorry - that's right. Hoping to *find* Jolly.

JOLLY: That's me.

MELISSA: You don't look very jolly.

JOLLY: I don't feel very jolly. Think of it - Snow White – cold, hungry and homeless., wandering through the wild wood searching vainly for me!

MELISSA: *(cheerfully)* Let's hope she doesn't get eaten by the big bad wolf.

JOLLY: WHAT!! / ROYAL SOOTHSAYER Woof Baa!

MELISSA: Didn't I tell you? Roaming through the woods is a big bad wolf!

ROYAL SOOTHSAYER: Woof Baa

MELISSA: It was very brave of me to come out here at all.

JOLLY: Oh heavens! We've got to find Snow White before that dreadful animal does.

ROYAL SOOTHSAYER: Let's hope we're not too late!

BLACKOUT AND MUSIC

SCENE 6 – THE ROYAL DRAWING ROOM

FX: thunder, lightning etc as WITCH enters

WITCH: You lot *still* here? What boring lives you must have! Now let me tell you – this scene is what we in the business call a filler. It doesn't advance the plot in any way, but is put in simply so the other actors can make costume changes……

So - for no reason at all I've come back to the palace to look for the Big Bad Wolf, though everyone knows - especially me - that he's up to no good in the woods.

Right….how shall we pass the time then? *(spots the apple)* Mmm – that looks a nice juicy apple. I rather fancy apples – I'm going to have a bit of that. What do you think? *(ad libs to audience – if they warn her about it being poisoned she poo poos them; if they encourage her to eat it she agrees with them. She takes a large bite.)*

Mmmm…lovely…… you can't beat a juicy red apple. *(She then makes a violent retching noise and falls to the ground apparently writhing in ludicrously O.T.T. agony until falling unconscious. For about three seconds. Whereupon she makes a miraculous recovery)*

Fooled you! You didn't really think I was dead did you? I told you I knew *everything*! I knew you *(pointing to one child)* watched too much television yesterday and you *(pointing to another)* didn't tidy your room before coming here. And I knew the apple was poisoned, so I magicked away the poison before I ate it. *(takes another bite)* Mmmm – delicious. A golden delicious. *(looks at watch)* Right – *(name of actor)* ……..should have got his wolf's head on by now. I'm off to rescue Snow White! See you shortly.

BLACKOUT AND MUSIC

SCENE 7 – A COTTAGE IN THE WILD WOOD

WOLF: Hello! Greetings everyone. I'm the big bad wolf. But you probably guessed that didn't you. It's my wolf's head – it's a bit of a giveaway. Do you like my cottage? Bedroom, kitchen, bathroom. All mod cons. A beautiful location slap bang in the middle of the Wild Wood. To be perfectly honest it's not - strictly speaking – *my* cottage. It belonged to a little old lady. But I ate her. Eating people is one of my hobbies actually. We all have hobbies, and that's mine. Eating people. Let me sing you a song about it. ………! *(calls technician's name)* Music please…..

Wolf's Song

CHORUS:
Wolf! Wolf! Wolf Wolf!

WOLF:
Let me tell you a story. I hope it won't be boring

Please be eager and alert; no drowsiness or snoring

'Cos I'm not the sort of fellow who cares to be ignored

I prefer to be applauded, to be worshipped and adored

'Cos I'm a wolf!

CHORUS:
Wolf! Wolf! Wolf! Wolf! Wolf!

WOLF:
I was wandering through the woods when I met this ancient lady

She told me that her name was Virginia O'Grady

I smiled at her and said she looked just like my dear Mummy

And thirty seconds later she was deep inside my tummy!

'Cos I'm a wolf!

CHORUS:
Wolf! Wolf! Wolf! Wolf! Wolf!

WOLF:
Some people like lamb chops, some people like fish

But for me there's really only the one satisfying dish

It's tender juicy kids that get my taste buds all a-flutter

Served with white wine, sauce and celery – and just a knob of butter
'Cos I'm a wolf!

CHORUS:
Wolf! Wolf! Wolf! Wolf! Wolf!

WOLF:
The moral of this story is really very clear
If you don't like being eaten , then you shouldn't come too near
For though I'm always very pleased to welcome and to greet you
I'm sorry but it won't be long before I'll have to eat you
'Cos I'm a wolf!

CHORUS:
Wolf! Wolf! Wolf! Wolf! Wolf!

(These lines spoken after music finishes)

WOLF: Who's afraid of the big bad wolf?

CHORUS: We are!

WOLF: *(turns to a child)* There. That was terrific wasn't it? What's your hobby son? Do you like eating people? No – quite right too. More for me that way. And don't even think about eating wolves! They taste horrid - far too much bone and gristle. Not like a tender juicy child eh? You look like a tasty morsel dear? Would you like to be eaten? My cousin went to Eton you know. *(SNOW WHITE is heard approaching from the foyer)*

Hey – who's that? Wow – it looks like my dinner has arrived, and I didn't even order it. *(He jumps into bed)*

SNOW WHITE: *(tentatively peering through door)* Hello?

WOLF: *(pretending to be a feeble old man)* Hello!

SNOW WHITE: Is there anybody there?

WOLF: *(losing his feebleness for a moment)* Well obviously yes – I've just said 'hello', haven't I?

SNOW: WHITE Hello?

WOLF: Exactly

SNOW WHITE: Would you mind if I came in?

WOLF: *(feeble again now)* Not at all my dear. Do come in. Excuse me if I don't get up – I'm feeling a little poorly.

SNOW WHITE: You're feeling your little *what*?

WOLF: Poorly! I'm feeling a little poorly…..

SNOW: WHITE Well I need to shelter from this storm *(FX storm)*

WOLF: *(out of character, to sound box)* Thanks *(name of Sound Operator)*. You were meant to play the storm at the *beginning* of the scene

SNOW WHITE: It's raining cats and dogs out there.

WOLF: How unpleasant! Miaow Woof! *(storm stops as suddenly as it started)* Ah….it seems to have stopped.

SNOW WHITE: *(surprised)* Oh yes….

WOLF: You just can't get the staff….

SNOW WHITE: *(shivering)* Anyway - I won't stay very long.

WOLF: Leave me to be the judge about that dear. *(beat)* Hold on a minute. Turn round. Don't I know you?

SNOW WHITE: I don't think so.

WOLF: What's your name? No - don't tell me. Give me a clue.

SNOW: Well….one of my names is a colour.

WOLF: Got it! You're Little Red Riding Hood!

SNOW WHITE: No. no. Wrong colour. I'm white, not red.

WOLF: Little *White* Riding Hood! Of course! Of course! I knew we'd met before.

SNOW WHITE: When was that?

WOLF: Shortly after you were born dear. Sadly I had an unfortunate misunderstanding with your mother and haven't seen you for 20 years. I'm your long-lost Uncle.

SNOW WHITE: Uncle who?

WOLF: Uncle Boris.

SNOW WHITE: I didn't know I had an Uncle Boris

SNOW WHITE

WOLF: You certainly do my dear. For Uncle Boris never lies…

SNOW WHITE: But you said we hadn't met for the last 20 years. How on earth did you recognise me?

WOLF: It's the way you walk dear. So unmistakably you. "That's my Little White Riding Hood as I live and breathe" I said to myself.

SNOW WHITE: But 20 years ago I was six months old. I couldn't walk; I could barely crawl.

WOLF: Look - let's not split hairs darling. For me you'll always be my Little White Riding Hood –

SNOW WHITE: Snow White actually.

WOLF: Snow White Riding Hood. Let's just be thankful that we've met after all this time. Come and give your Uncle Boris a big hug.

SNOW WHITE: *(approaching bed)* My goodness – what big ears you've got Uncle Boris!

WOLF: All the better to hear you with my dear

SNOW WHITE: And what big eyes you've got!

WOLF: All the better to see you with my dear,

SNOW WHITE: And what big teeth you've got!

Beat. WOLF smiles at audience….

WOLF: Yes, they are a bit big aren't they. I need to find a good dentist to file them down. *(beat)* But…… they do have their advantages you know.

SNOW WHITE: What's that?

WOLF: *(jumping out of bed)* They're all the better to *eat* you with!

WITCH: *(appearing from nowhere)* Not so fast Wolf! *(fx spell WOLF freezes)*

SNOW WHITE: He's a *wolf*?!

WITCH: Of course he's a wolf. Look at his head for heaven's sake.

SNOW WHITE: Oh yes! You're right! And who are you?

WITCH: I'm a witch – and I've not only saved your life Snow White, but I've rescued the whole community from this monstrously evil wolf, who eats people as a hobby.

SNOW WHITE: Don't be too hard on him. He's my Uncle Boris.

WITCH: And I'm the Tooth Fairy.

SNOW WHITE: Really? I thought you said you were a witch.

WITCH: *(exasperated)* Do I look like the Tooth Fairy?

SNOW WHITE: I've never met the Tooth Fairy.

WITCH: Well I'm not. I'm a witch. And I'm taking this wolf back to the palace to let King Horace deal with him. *(FX spell. The WOLF is released from the restraining spell)* Right you – you're coming with me. And no trying to escape or I'll turn you into a tuna fish sandwich….

WOLF: Can't I persuade you to stay for a glass of sherry before we leave? An Amontillado. It's very good. Quite dry but -

WITCH: You can't sweet-talk your way out of this Wolf! We're off to the palace – and by nightfall, if I have my way, you'll be barbecued wolf!

WOLF: *(looks at audience)* Woof. Baa!

BLACKOUT AND MUSIC.

SCENE 8 – THE ROYAL DRAWING ROOM

KING: *(surprised to sees audience)* Ah hello, Just having a muffin. You can't beat them you know. Some people prefer – no, no, hold on I've said all that already, haven't I. Have I sung you my muffin song? *(audience: yes)* Would you like to hear it again.

MIRROR: No we wouldn't!

KING: *(hurt)* Be like that. Don't you just hate talking mirrors! *(to MIRROR)* You're just a big pane, that's what you are! *(beat)* Now – where's my twin brother the Royal Soothsayer? I've been waiting for half an hour for him to turn up. Not that I'll get any sense out of him. All he says nowadays is 'Hippopotamus Woof Baa!" *(pause. KING vainly waits for a non-appearing MELISSA. Raises his voice)* I said: "All he says nowadays is 'Hippopotamus Woof Baa!"

MELISSA: *(enters triumphantly)* All is well. Snow White has been rescued and the thousand gold coins have been found! *(hopefully a round of applause from audience)*

KING: Terrific news Meriam! That's made me jolly!

MELISSA: I don't think so Sire

KING: What do you mean?

MELISSA: Well Jolly's in the corridor waiting to see you.

KING: *(confused)* Er…right. Send him in! *(She goes. Almost immediately the WITCH enters, with the WOLF dragging behind)*

WITCH: Horace!

KING: My goodness Jolly you've changed! Another growing spurt? You look just my sister's cousin, the Witch.

WITCH: I am the Witch you fool!

KING: Of course you are. Silly me. What brings you to the palace Bertha?

WITCH: This wolf Horace. Come here you.

WOLF: I am here. *(and he is)*

KING: How do you do.

WOLF: A great pleasure to meet you your Majesty!

KING: The pleasure's all mine Wolf.

WOLF: Do call me Boris

KING: Certainly Wolf

WOLF: I've heard so much about you. Your great wisdom; your charitable deeds; your love of muffins.

KING: What a well-mannered animal! Wolves on the whole have a bit of a bad name round here.

WITCH: Horace don't be ridiculous. This wolf eats people!

KING: Well - nobody's perfect

WITCH: He tried to eat Snow White!

WOLF: *(correcting her)* Snow White Riding Hood

KING: Where *is* Snow White? I've thrown her appalling aunt out of the palace for poisoning apples, but her niece has disappeared .

WITCH: She's fine Horace. She came back to the palace with me. Though I'm not sure where she is now.

KING: *(calling)* Melinda!

MELISSA: *(appearing)* Were you calling *me* My Liege?

KING: Ask Snow White to come and see me will you. And while you're at it tell Jolly and my brother to pop in as well.

MELISSA: *(thinks about this)* Er….that may be a bit difficult.

KING: What do you mean difficult? It's a Royal Command Marigold. Obey it at once!

MELISSA: *(defiantly)* I can't.

KING: What?

WITCH: Horace. Horace….think about it for a moment will you?

KING: Think about what? I'm not a great fan of thinking.

WOLF: We could only afford *four* actors…remember?

KING: *(struggling)* Yes?

MELISSA: And that's us four…..

WITCH: And there are eight characters in the play -

WOLF: *Seven* of whom appear in this scene…

Beat the KING thinks about this. Lightbulb moment.

KING: Ahh....see what you mean. Bit tricky eh?

MELISSA: So what are we going to do Sire?

KING: Er......We use our initiative. Needs must when the devil drives.

MELISSA: Pardon?

KING: Watch this. *(He changes hats and becomes the ROYAL SOOTHSAYER)* Ah my Lord, my Liege, wonderful news. We've found the 1000 gold coins!

KING: *(changing hats)* Jolly good!

ROYAL SOOTHSAYER: *(changing hats – this continues every time they speak)* Yes! Nobody else found it! Just us. Jolly and Me. Certainly not Melissa.

KING: Who's Melissa? Do I know this person??

ROYAL SOOTHSAYER: Hippopotamus Woof Baa!

MELISSA: I'm Melissa. I'm also *(quick change)* Snow White.

JOLLY: *(removing Wolf's head)* And I'm Jolly. *(putting it back)* Though I'm also the Wolf

ROYAL SOOTHSAYER: Woof, Baa

KING: What was that?

ROYAL SOOTHSAYER: It was me Sire. Any mention of an animal....

WOLF: Like a wolf -

ROYAL SOOTHSAYER: Woof Baa

WITCH: And he says -

ROYAL SOOTHSAYER: Woof Baa

KING: Ah yes! I remember.

WITCH: All my own work you know! And when one says a word beginning with 'P' –

ROYAL SOOTHSAYER: Hippopotamus Woof Baa!

WITCH: That's what happens.

KING: Oh dear!

ROYAL SOOTHSAYER: Woof Baa.

KING: What?

JOLLY: It's an animal you see – Deer.

ROYAL SOOTHSAYER: Woof Baa.

WOLF: Very tasty, deer!

ROYAL SOOTHSAYER: Woof Baa!

KING: Tasty?

WOLF: Especially eaten with gravy and roast potatoes

ROYAL SOOTHSAYER: Hippopotamus Woof Baa

KING: Will you stop saying that. Please!

ROYAL SOOTHSAYER: Hippopotamus Woof Baa

KING: I can't *bear* this -

ROYAL SOOTHSAYER: Woof Baa-

KING: *Be Quiet!*

   (Beat)

KING: Perfect!

ROYAL SOOTHSAYER: Hippopotamus, Woof, Baa

   (Pause while they draw breath)

JOLLY: My Liege I have a favour to ask you

KING: Ask away!

JOLLY: Once I have received my gold coin would it be possible….

ROYAL SOOTHSAYER: Hippopotamus Woof Baa -

JOLLY: To ask you for the hand of Snow White.

MELISSA: That's me! *(then realises she is MELISSA – changes wigs)* No it's not.

SNOW WHITE: *That's* me!

KING: You want her hand?

JOLLY: If it is the King's pleasure. *(MELISSA seizes ROYAL*

SOOTHSAYER'S hat by mistake and becomes him)

MELISSA: Hippopotamus Woof Baa.

KING: You'll need more than her hand, my boy. I know about these things. Promise.

MELISSA: *(still wearing ROYAL SOOTHSAYER'S hat)* Hippopotamus Woof Baa.

(Pace gets quicker and quicker from here on)

KING: What do you think Snowy? For you, is he the right person?

ROYAL SOOTHSAYER: *(grabbing hat back)* Hippopotamus Woof Baa

SNOW WHITE: For me Sire, he's the *only* person.

ROYAL SOOTHSAYER: Hippopotamus Woof Baa.

KING: Then I'm pleased –

WITCH: *(seizes Royal Soothsayer's hat)* Hippopotamus Woof Baa

KING: - to grant your request my dear -

ROYAL SOOTHSAYER: *(seizing his hat back from the WITCH)* Woof Baa

MELISSA: *(changing wigs)* Oh! How romantic….

JOLLY: I shall love and cherish you for ever Melissa!

SNOW WHITE: *(correcting him)* Snow White.

JOLLY: Snow White

WOLF: You lucky dog!

ROYAL SOOTHSAYER: Woof Baa.

KING: Pardon?

ROYAL SOOTHSAYER: Hippopotamus Woof Baa -

JOLLY: I'm the happiest man in the palace -

ROYAL SOOTHSAYER: Hippopotamus Woof Baa -

KING: Yes – well -

MELISSA: What a joyous picture!

ROYAL SOOTHSAYER: Hippopotamus Woof Baa-

KING: Will you stop that -

WITCH: I personally -

ROYAL SOOTHSAYER: Hippopotamus Woof Baa -

KING: Can you please-

ROYAL SOOTHSAYER: Hippopotamus Woof Baa-

SNOW WHITE: My precious!

ROYAL SOOTHSAYER: Hippopotamus Woof Baa!

KING: Look can we –

JOLLY: You're perfection!

ROYAL SOOTHSAYER: Hippopotamus Woof Baa -

KING: *(exploding)* That's quite enough! Stop it! STOP IT ALL OF YOU! *(They all come to an exhausted halt)*

ALL: Sorry….

PAUSE

KING: Look – Melissa -

MELISSA: *(astonished)* You got my name right!

KING: Please escort Snow White to her chamber to freshen up.

MELISSA: Right away my Liege!

SNOW WHITE: Thank you Sire. *(to JOLLY)* I can hardly wait for our marriage darling – after which I shall be Snow Jolly!! *(rest of cast groan)*

MELISSA: This way my Lady.

SNOW WHITE: Thank you Melissa. *(They leave)*

KING: And as for you brother -

ROYAL SOOTHSAYER: Yes My Liege.

KING: I'd like to congratulate both you and Jilly here for finding Uncle Horatio's thousand gold coins.

ROYAL SOOTHSAYER: Another one of my prophecies - Hippopotamus Woof Baa - to hit the nail directly on the head eh?

KING: What nail? What head? Sounds painful.

ROYAL SOOTHSAYER: Hippopotamus Woof Baa.

JOLLY: *(to ROYAL SOOTHSAYER)* Well – it was actually Melissa, wasn't it, who personally -

ROYAL SOOTHSAYER: *(as in "shut up")* Hippopotamus Woof Baa!

JOLLY: Sorry.

KING: Now then you two - why don't you go and celebrate in the Royal Bar. Have one on me!

ROYAL SOOTHSAYER: Thank you my Liege! This way Jolly!

JOLLY: Right away.

The two walk off and come back immediately as the KING and the WOLF

WOLF: And here we are again.

KING: Er… Right… *(working it out)* That leaves just you Bertha…

WITCH: Yes

KING: Me …. Er…and….

WOLF: Me. Boris. But I'm afraid I must be going now Sire. I've got dinner to catch.

WITCH: You're going nowhere Wolf. Horace – this animal needs to be executed immediately.

KING: I say – that's a bit harsh isn't it Bertha? A sad way to end such a lovely day.

WOLF: I couldn't agree more.

WITCH: He's a menace to mankind.

WOLF: Nonsense! I'm just a sad, lonely, misunderstood wolf Sire. I'm a sheep in wolf's clothing!

KING: I'll tell you what. Let's put it to the audience. When I count to three, if you want me to save the wolf, I want you to shout "Save the Wolf" at the top of your voices.

WITCH: And if you want the wolf executed please shout "Barbecue Boris " as loudly as you can.

KING: Got it? "Save the Wolf" or "Barbecue Norris!"

WITCH/WOLF: Boris.

KING: Boris

WOLF: *(politely to audience)* I just want to say, by the way, that if anyone shouts 'Barbecue Boris', I'll eat you.

KING: Right then….One, Two, *Three!*

The audience shout their verdicts

KING: Sorry, sorry, I didn't quite get that. Again please, but louder!

The audience shout again. The loudest audience voice to be heard now is the WOLF'S who has joined them in the audience and is screaming 'Save the wolf'!

KING: Well – that seems pretty clear to me. The wolf is saved. Well done my boy!

WITCH: That's ridiculous! The Wolf was in the audience shouting louder than anybody.

KING: Was he? Well that shows splendid initiative if you ask me. Well done Doris!

WOLF: *(bowing)* Thank you Your Royal Highness

KING: Now I think we should end the play by all singing a jolly song. Anybody know any jolly songs?

WOLF: I know a great one. It's very jolly – and it's all about me. And the audience can join in with the "wolf" bits!

KING: Excellent, excellent

MELISSA: My Liege -

KING: Ah, Meriam – you can sing along with us. Off you go Wolf!

Wolf's Song (Reprise)

CHORUS:
Wolf! Wolf! Wolf Wolf!

WOLF:
Let me tell you a story. I hope it won't be boring
Please be eager and alert; no drowsiness or snoring
'Cos I'm not the sort of fellow who cares to be ignored
I prefer to be applauded, to be worshipped and adored
'Cos I'm a wolf!

CHORUS:
Wolf! Wolf! Wolf! Wolf! Wolf!

WOLF:
I was wandering through the woods, when I met this ancient lady
She told me that her name was Virginia O'Grady
I smiled at her and said she looked just like my dear Mummy
And thirty seconds later she was deep inside my tummy!
'Cos I'm a wolf!

CHORUS:
Wolf! Wolf! Wolf! Wolf! Wolf!

WOLF:
Some people like lamb chops, some people like fish
But for me there's really only the one satisfying dish
It's tender juicy kids that get my taste buds all a-flutter
Served with white wine, sauce and celery – and just a knob of butter
'Cos I'm a wolf!

CHORUS:
Wolf! Wolf! Wolf! Wolf! Wolf!

WOLF:
The moral of this story is really very clear
If you don't like being eaten , then you shouldn't come too near
For though I'm always very pleased to welcome and to greet you
I'm sorry but it won't be long before I'll have to eat you
'Cos I'm a wolf!

CHORUS:
Wolf! Wolf! Wolf! Wolf! Wolf!

(These lines spoken after music finishes)

WOLF: Who's afraid of the big bad wolf?

CHORUS: We are!

KING: Well wasn't that jolly! Right then – it's time for you lot to toddle off home – but before you go a word of advice from someone who knows a bit about life.

WOLF/WITCH/MELISSA: What's that?

KING: Keep well away from wolves if at all possible!
ALL : Hippopotamus Woof Baa!

CURTAIN

ABOUT THE AUTHOR

Gordon House

Gordon House joined the BBC as a Studio Manager in 1972, and worked in Children's Television and Radio Sport, before becoming a Radio Drama director. He headed the small BBC World Service Drama team for fourteen years, during which time the Unit won over thirty national and international awards - many of them plays directed by Gordon himself. He initiated the World International Playwriting Competition for radio dramatists, run in conjunction with the British Council, and also wrote a monthly humorous column for the World Service magazine "BBC On Air" under the pseudonym "Nelson Mature".

Gordon has twice adjudicated the National Theatre Awards in Zimbabwe; run Shakespeare workshops in Kenya and Uganda, been a guest lecturer for the Radio Nederland overseas drama course and produced a Shakespeare revue for the Harare International Festival of Arts. He has directed several plays in conjunction with the Canadian Broadcasting Company and with LA Theatre Works, Los Angeles. In 1998 he won the Writers' Guild Special Prize for services for his work with new writers, and two years later won the Sony Drama Award for Best Drama with his World Service production of Alpha by Mike Walker. He was a founder member, and ex-Chair, of The Worldplay Group a radio association of drama directors from broadcasting stations around the world. In April 2001 he became Head of BBC Radio Drama, a post which he held until his retirement from the BBC in March 2005. He was a judge at Prix Italia and Prix Europa conventions, and his tenure as Head culminated in the Department winning its largest ever number of international awards in a single year.

Since retiring from the BBC, Gordon has freelanced as a producer, teacher, and drama consultant. He has taught Radio Drama and run Radio Masterclasses at ALRA, Arts Ed, Bristol, Central, Drama Studio, East 15, Rose Burford and RWCMD. He was a drama consultant in Guyana for the Aids-based soap Opera, Merundoi and continues to direct occasional radio plays for the BBC as an Independent producer. In 2010 he was voted Radio Drama Producer of the Year by the Radio Academy. Gordon has more recently written the four family pantomimes printed in this book and staged at Colour House Theatre in Merton. He directed three of them himself. He also wrote and directed a radio play for the BBC in 2024 – Rumpelstiltskin's Radio

ABOUT THE AUTHOR

Drama Romance – about a radio producer's hapless attempt to direct one of these plays as a Radio 4 Drama.

Gordon is married with two children, and three granddaughters. When not working, or babysitting, he plays golf – very badly. He was the Centenary Captain of Wimbledon Common Golf Club in 2008 and is currently Vice-President of the club, and Secretary of their Senior Section the WAGGS - the Wimbledon Ageless Gentlemen Golfers. His "hilarious" (his description) autobiography "Pea Brain from Radio 4" remains unpublished in a bottom drawer. As an agent memorably said to him "Celebrity memoirs are a hard sell Gordon – and let's face it, you're not a celebrity….."

Also by Gordon House:

Snow White & the Big Bad Wolf - and other stories.
ISBN: 978-1-7393020-9-2

Published by Beercott Books

www.ingramcontent.com/pod-product-compliance
Lightning Source LLC
Chambersburg PA
CBHW061727070526
44583CB00024B/3040